THE COMPLETE GRIMOIRE

The Complete Grimoire

Magickal Practices and Spells for
Awakening Your Inner Witch

Lidia Pradas,
Creator of Wiccan Tips

First Published in 2020 by Fair Winds Press, an imprint of The Quarto Group,
100 Cummings Center, Suite 265-D, Beverly, MA 01915, USA.
T (978) 282-9590 F (978) 283-2742 Quarto.com

24 10

ISBN: 978-1-59233-970-9

Digital edition published in 2020
eISBN: 978-1-63159-905-7

Library of Congress Cataloging-in-Publication Data

Names: Pradas, Lidia, author.
Title: The complete grimoire : practices for awakening your inner witch / Lidia Pradas.
Description: Beverly : Fairwinds Press, 2020. | Includes index. | Summary: "The Complete Grimoire is a practical and authentic guide for the beginning witchcraft practitioner by the creator of the hugely popular Instagram handle Wiccan Tips"-- Provided by publisher.
Identifiers: LCCN 2020002534 | ISBN 9781592339709 (trade paperback) | ISBN 9781631599057 (ebook)
Subjects: LCSH: Witchcraft. | Magic. | Herbals.
Classification: LCC BF1566 .P69 2020 | DDC 133.4/3--dc23
LC record available at https://lccn.loc.gov/2020002534

Cover design: Tanya Jacobson, crsld.co
Illustration: Nata Vedana

Printed in China

To all who have accompanied me
during this journey,
making this dream possible.

Contents

WELCOME

Introduction

Welcome to my grimoire! You are about to begin an exciting journey of ancient knowledge and self-discovery. In this book, I share with you everything you need to know about the pillars of witchcraft, helping you connect with the energy of the universe. Let me guide you through this path of the occult!

My name is Lidia and I was born in Spain, where we still keep some of our ancient pagan traditions. I have always felt a calling to learn more about my ancestors, and I enjoy visiting archeological sites where I can connect with my Celtiberian roots. My mother began teaching me about the energy of the universe when it became clear at an early age that I had a special sensitivity to energies.

As I grew up, I was curious about the occult and I started reading books and attending courses, choosing the Wiccan path several years ago. I also have a deep connection with Mother Earth and environmental awareness, and this led me to earn a bachelor's degree in environmental science. I wrote this book for all types of witches, but you may notice my beliefs coming through, especially those related to protecting Mother Earth.

This book is a concise and in-depth guide of how to practice witchcraft. This includes practicing meditation and divination, connecting with Mother Earth, setting up an altar, using herbs and crystals, celebrating the pagan holidays, working with deities and spirits, casting spells, and much more!

This is my personal grimoire, and I included everything that I consider important for my craft. You will learn the basic principles of the craft and how to incorporate them into your life. At the end of each chapter, you will find a section titled "Things I Wish Somebody Had Told Me," where you will find my personal advice and anecdotes to help you as you find and travel your own path.

Everybody has the potential to use witchcraft. In these pages, you will learn how to work with your energy and intention, as well as the energy of the elements that surround you. This book is a tool that can help you bring truth and power to your life through communion with the universe. Let's get started, and let's awaken your inner witch!

CHAPTER 1

Witchcraft FAQs

Here I answer some of the most common concerns people have as they begin to learn about witchcraft. If you already know the answers to these questions, skip to chapter 2.

What Is Witchcraft?

Pagans have practiced witchcraft since ancient times, but, sadly, witchcraft is a misunderstood practice in today's society. The way witches are represented in pop culture is pretty distant from reality, and there have been several attempts by some religions to erase pagan rituals altogether.

In this universe, we are all connected through invisible and multidimensional links. You can imagine this as a network of invisible threads that join every spirit, including yours. Magick creates new patterns in this network, generating subtle changes in our destiny.

Dion Fortune, a British occultist from the beginning of the twentieth century, explained it this way: "Magic . . . is a technique for the utilization and direction of the astral forces, which are the immediate causes behind the world of appearances." Astral forces are part of an intangible realm and a part of the mundane world, a part of ourselves. To put it in her words: "The mastery of these powers is based upon self-mastery."

Some people look to witchcraft to reveal ancient secrets. The truth is that a deeper understanding of yourself and the forces of the universe are revelations that *only you* can achieve through your personal spirit, working and reconnecting with Mother Nature. Your path will lead you to transformation, self-discovery, and a return to the roots of humankind.

Can Anybody Practice Witchcraft?

Yes, absolutely. Each person has the necessary elements within themselves to practice witchcraft. Some people are born with special abilities that make it easier for them to practice witchcraft—but all those skills can be developed with dedication and the right techniques.

In the end, witchcraft is a choice. If you are born into a family of witches and decide not to practice, you are not a witch. If you aren't born into a family of witches but you do decide to practice, you are a witch.

Witchcraft doesn't belong to any particular group. That said, some cultures and religions include witchcraft in their practices, and witchcraft is deeply enmeshed in their broader belief systems. As witches, we need to show respect for these traditions and not appropriate or "borrow" the rituals for our own use (see "Smoke Cleansing vs. Smudging" on page 104).

What's the Difference Between Paganism, Wicca, and Witchcraft?

Paganism is an umbrella term for different religions that worship the earth and ancient deities.

Wicca is a neo-pagan religion. It has some rules, rituals, and ethics to follow, such as the Wheel of the Year (see chapter 3) and the Wiccan rede, or moral code: *An ye harm none, do what ye will.*

Witchcraft is a practice. It is a tool that can be used as you prefer, guided by your own morals and ethics. You don't need to be Wiccan to practice witchcraft. And, in some branches of Wicca, you don't need to practice witchcraft to be Wiccan.

To simplify it, all Wiccans are pagans, but not all pagans are Wiccans. Most Wiccans are witches, but not all witches are Wiccans. Some pagans are witches, and some witches are pagans.

There are many paths out there. I encourage you to explore your spirituality. Find what you are drawn to and follow the path that best suits you.

Do I Need a Coven to Practice Witchcraft?

No. By definition, a coven is a group of witches who voluntarily practice together following specific rules. There are different types of covens drawing upon different traditions, and, as with any activity group, they also depend on the personalities of the members. Belonging to a coven is a personal decision that works for some witches and doesn't work for others. There are pros and cons to both options.

Keep in mind that choosing the solitary path does not mean always being alone. There are open circles that welcome solitary witches to celebrate rituals or sabbats. And you can always have witchy friends and learn and practice with them without having to be in a coven.

COVEN		SOLITARY PATH	
Pros	**Cons**	**Pros**	**Cons**
It is more structured.	You have to respect the rules.	You have more freedom.	You can get lonely.
You make friends who will help you when you need it.	You have to adapt to scheduled dates for meetings.	You only work on what interests you and learn at your own pace.	It may be more difficult to find guidance when you need it.
You may learn faster because there are people teaching you.	You may not get along with all the members.	You practice with other people only in the ways you want to.	You are responsible for all of the planning, scheduling, buying supplies, etc.

Can I Practice a Religion and Be a Witch?

Yes, at least from the point of view of witchcraft. Witchcraft does not tie you to any deity, ritual, or ethic, so it is compatible with all religions. Some religions staunchly oppose witchcraft, making *them* incompatible with the craft—but not the other way around.

What's the Male Term for Witch?

The male term for witch is, in fact, witch. Witch is a gender-neutral term, but it has been associated primarily with women. It is true that male witches were common in some places. For example, in the Middle Ages, in Moscow, male witches significantly outnumbered female witches. And during the medieval persecution of witches in Normandy, more men than women were accused of witchcraft.

That said, throughout the ages it has been common for the term *witch* to be used against women. Labeling women as witches was a way to control them and prevent them from accessing professions such as medicine. Women also were targeted frequently during witch hunts when being accused of witchcraft brought suffering and even death.

What Are the Most Common Types of Witches?

Sometimes witches are classified by type, depending on how they live their craft. Remember, though, that each path is different, so you don't need to fit into any of these categories—or even into just one category.

COSMIC WITCH Cosmic witches base their craft on the energy of the cosmos. They use astrology and astronomy to cast their rituals, and they feel a special connection with celestial bodies. Timing is very important to them, as they match their activities to celestial events.

ECLECTIC WITCH Eclectic witches do not follow a single path or tradition: they create their own. They choose rituals, deities, and spells from different traditions, depending on what works for them and what does not.

GREEN WITCH Green witches have a strong connection with Mother Earth. They are drawn to growing and using their own herbs in their craft. Walks in nature are their favorite way to ground themselves and connect with their magick. They are very interested in the medicinal properties of different herbs and make their own brews and potions.

HEREDITARY WITCH A witch who was born into a family of witches is a hereditary witch. Witchcraft is in their lineage, and rituals, spells, and knowledge are handed down from one generation to another. These family traditions are typically unique and outsiders are rarely included.

KITCHEN WITCH Kitchen witches mix their cooking skills with their rituals. They infuse their food with intent and charge their dishes with magick. Usually, these witches have an in-depth knowledge of the composition and properties of food. Kitchen witchcraft, along with green witchcraft, is one of the crafts that focuses more on the mundane world.

SECULAR WITCH A witch whose craft is separate from their spirituality is a secular witch. They don't work with deities or worship them. Their witchcraft is based on their skills and tools, such as candles, herbs, or crystals. This doesn't mean that all secular witches are atheists; some of them are religious. It means that their religious path is fully differentiated from their witchcraft path.

SOLITARY WITCH A witch who doesn't belong to a coven is a solitary witch. They practice alone by their own choice or because of their circumstances. Their craft tends to be more personal, as they only work on what really interests them.

WICCAN WITCH A witch who is also a Wiccan follows the Wiccan rules and rituals as a part of their magick and spirituality. There are many branches of Wicca, each with their own rituals, deities, etc. Some examples include Gardnerian Wicca, Alexandrian Wicca, Celtic Wicca, and Dianic Wicca.

CHAPTER 2

First Steps

Now it is time to find and walk your path! When faced with this first step, many of us say, "I want to begin, but . . ." We can list countless reasons *not* to start: I don't have time to master witchcraft; I don't know where to start; I need to do something else first. These are common thoughts in all of us, not only about witchcraft but about life in general.

Change only starts when we realize that the perfect moment does not exist. The present is always an opportunity to work toward our goals. There will always be more things to do and more lessons to learn. That's exactly why now is the time to start. In witchcraft, we learn, we grow, and we find help to walk through life.

This chapter covers concepts and terminology that may be difficult at first. But, at the same time, it is the most important chapter of the book because it explains the fundamentals of how witchcraft operates. I've tried my best to make it concise, comprehensive, and easy to read. Take notes as you go and highlight the parts that you feel are most important or that you want to research further. Remember that this is a journey, and there is so much to learn along the way.

Mother Earth, the Energy of the Universe, and the Five Elements

Humans have always had a strong connection with Mother Earth. She was worshiped as a life-giving entity, and she was revered and protected. Over time, technology usurped her place and has left us orphaned and desolate.

It can be difficult to understand the bond that ancient humans had with nature—and even more difficult to restore it. But it is not impossible, and we long to get it back. When we walk outdoors, we can still experience a warm feeling of coming home. It is almost nostalgic, and it fills us with energy and soothes our spirits. Mother Earth welcomes us with her open arms, and when we are in her embrace, we realize what we have lost.

Witches have a strong connection with Mother Earth. She is the origin of our life and power, and we will return to her when our cycle—of birth, life, and death—is complete. Like a loving mother, she is our home and our protector. We owe her respect and care. It is through our spiritual awakening that we are each able to develop and restore our connection with her, allowing us to feel and use her energy.

Taoist philosophy considers Nature to be a perfect being. Mother Nature has her two opposite and interdependent forces or energies: yin and yang. These two energies consume each other and regenerate themselves continually, always returning to balance after a disturbance. The tai chi symbol is the representation of these interactions, a dynamic balance that creates the universe from nothingness.

In this book, I refer to "negative" energies. It is important to understand that this means energies are unbalanced. It does not mean that yin or yang is harmful energy. Opposing energies are necessary and complementary, and problems arise when they are not in balance.

Yin and yang originate from a holistic energy that is present throughout the universe. This energy has different names in different cultures: the Chinese call it Chi, and the Japanese call it Ki. In this book, I refer to it as "inner energy," as it is inside of everything—it forms part of everything.

In the Taoist tradition, telluric energy emanates from the earth, and the sky emits cosmic energy. The telluric energy is yin, and the cosmic energy is yang. The interaction of these two forces is

THE FIVE ELEMENTS	
Chinese Approach	**Occidental Approach**
Wood, Fire, Earth, Metal, and Water	Fire, Water, Air, Earth, and Spirit

THE PENTACLE WITH THE FIVE ELEMENTS AND THEIR SYMBOLS

ELEMENT	DIRECTION	COLOR	SYMBOL	INFLUENCE AREA	ALTAR REPRESENTATIONS
Fire	South	Red	Upward triangle	Passion, courage, love, energy, strength, inspiration	Candles, dragons, salamanders, hot spices, lanterns
Water	West	Blue	Downward triangle	Intuition, emotions, healing, dreams	Crystals, mirrors, sea-shells, chalices
Air	East	Yellow	Upward triangle crossed by a line	Communication, law, knowledge, language, movement	Bells, music, feathers, scents
Earth	North	Green/ Brown	Downward triangle crossed by a line	Fertility, stability, hard work, resiliency, family	Soil, wood, crystals, plants, animal representations
Spirit	Center	Purple	Circle	Witchcraft, connection, psychic abilities, spirit realm	Circles, wheels, spirals, webs

further divided into five stages or elements. There are some important differences in the way the Chinese tradition and ancient occidental cultures approach these elements.

My tradition is Celtiberian, and it is influenced by occidental practices. Ancient Celts believed in three main elements: earth, fire, and water. These were represented in the triquetra, or "trinity knot," which is deeply interrelated with the three life states in their belief system: life, death, and rebirth. Ancient Greeks divided the universe into five elements: fire, water, air, earth, and ether or quintessence. Nowadays, in many occidental witchcraft practices, the element of ether has been substituted with the element of spirit.

Everything around us, including us, is made from the five elements. The elements work together, and the fifth element, the spirit, is what allows the other four to function in unison. At the same time, the spirit is also a part of the universe it helps create. An easy way to visualize this concept is to imagine the fifth element as the web that connects everything.

Although the five elements work collectively, each one has different correspondences. The elements are usually represented by the symbol of the pentacle, a five-pointed star surrounded by a circle. Each point of the star represents one of the elements, linked by one unique line. The circle embodies the line of life, one that has no beginning or end. The pentacle has become a powerful symbol that represents a belief system and also contains the energy of the universe as a whole.

Witchcraft is strongly related to the natural processes that occur in our bodies, planet, and universe. Personally, I encourage all witches to learn the science behind nature: the cycle of the seasons, the phases of the moon, the rhythm of the tides, and so on. A deeper understanding of these natural events allows us to use our energy more effectively.

Inner Energy and How to Project It

The universe is formed by energies and their interactions and so is our body. The relationship between the yin and yang in the human body is complex and creates a unique polarity in each person.

Chi is the vital energy or "inner energy" that serves as a source for yin and yang. Our bodies have the ability to generate it. This ability starts with a sparkle transmitted from our parents at conception. It is developed until adolescence and then it gradually decreases until the time of natural death. When we die, we run out of vital energy and are transformed into other types of energies as we return to Mother Earth.

Living requires inner energy. Think of it as the fuel that allows us to function. There are some activities that consume more inner energy than others. For example, unhealthy eating habits, mental and physical exhaustion, illness, overindulging, and the natural effects of aging all decrease the amount of inner energy in our bodies.

The body consumes inner energy—and it also creates it. According to Traditional Chinese Medicine, Chi is created in the point named *dan tian*, located in the center-lower belly. Dan tian is translated as "elixir field," and it works like a generator of inner energy, nurtured by the yin and yang energies that emanate from the earth and the sky. Dan tian is divided into three smaller points—lower, middle, and upper dan tian. This division allows humans to receive, create, and metabolize Chi.

To stay healthy, we should maintain a continual and steady flow of inner energy throughout the body. Traditional Chinese Medicine states that each organ is influenced by yin or yang energy, and our organs are connected through energy channels called meridians. There are twelve principal meridians in the body that allow the energy to flow within us. Fifteen collateral meridians connect the principal ones and the organs, and eight extraordinary meridians are reservoirs of energy.

There are many disciplines that base their exercises on the meridian network. For example, qi gong stretches, moves, and flexes the body's channels; acupuncture and acupressure manipulate specific points located in the meridians to help correct imbalances in energy flow.

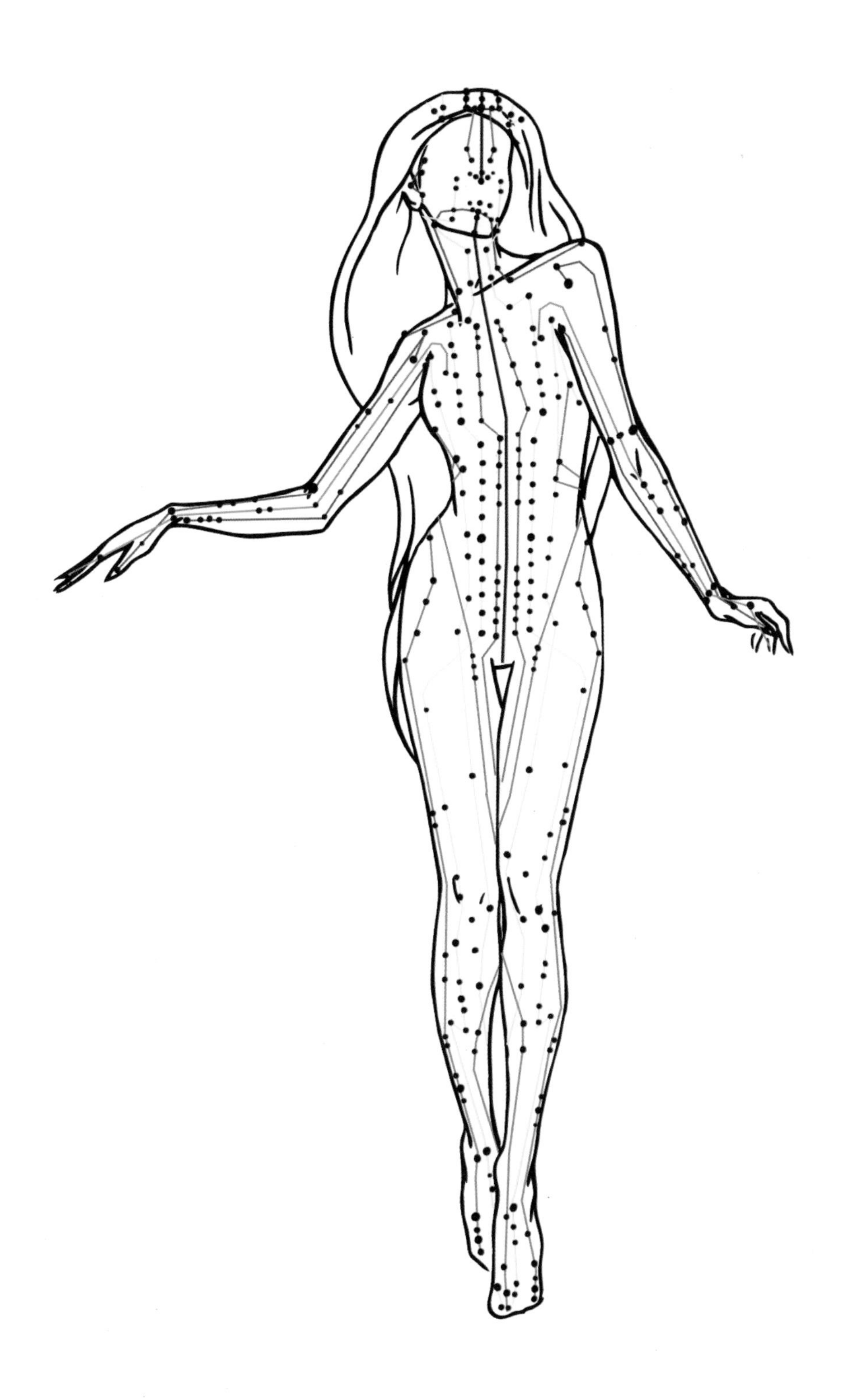

Chakras and Meridians

Chakra means "wheel" or "circle" in Sanskrit. It refers to energy points in the body that allow us to manage energy. Acupuncture points and meridians are also vital for energy flow, and they usually coincide in location with chakras. For example, at the top of the head we can find the *bai hui* point, and it matches the location of the crown chakra.

Despite their similarities, chakras and acupuncture points are not the same. Think of chakras as gates that allow us to project and receive energy. Acupuncture points are part of a circuit.

Activating and opening our chakras allows us to consciously receive and send energy to the universe. When we have finished our energy work, we should close our chakras, except for the root chakra and the crown chakra. These should remain a bit open to receive the yin and yang from the earth and the sky, respectively. Opening, activating, and closing your chakras is a complex exercise that takes time and practice to master. Leaving your chakras open may cause you to be more sensitive to the energy of other people.

Our bodies absorb energy from our surroundings and release the energy that no longer serves us back to the earth. This type of "used" energy does not hurt Mother Earth, as it is part of her natural cycle (in a similar way the CO_2 released from our breathing doesn't hurt her). Everything that is alive receives and releases energy during its lifetime, recycling it. Humans do pollute the environment with their actions, but not with their energies.

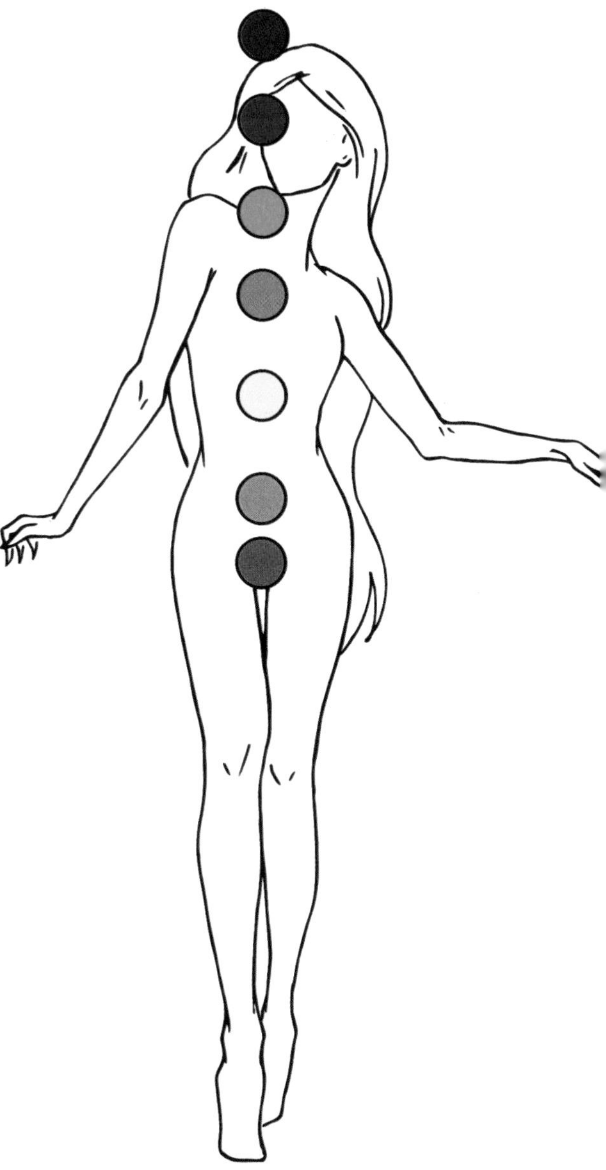

NUMBER	CHAKRA	COLOR	CORRESPONDENCES
1st	Root	Red	Survival, grounding, primitive needs, physical needs
2nd	Sacral	Orange	Emotional balance, sexuality, joy, pleasure
3rd	Solar Plexus	Yellow	Self-will, identity, self-confidence, manifestation
4th	Heart	Green	Love, compassion, hope, forgiveness, healing
5th	Throat	Blue	Communication, self-expression, truth, inner voice
6th	Third Eye	Indigo	Psychic abilities, intuition, visualization, extrasensory perception, wisdom, creativity
7th	Crown	Violet	Spirituality, connection with the universe, enlightenment

Breathing, Meditating, Grounding, and Visualization

These techniques are the basis of witchcraft, because they allow us to know and control our mind, body, and spirit.

Breathing

Breathing is the physical way that the body has to restore the inner energy that it loses during daily activities. Correct breathing should first fill the abdomen, then the thorax, and finally the zone of the collarbone. This should be natural, not done in a forced or methodical way. Think of the way a calm baby breathes: the body inflates like a small balloon, combining abdominal and thoracic breathing. This is the most complete and perfect way of breathing.

Babies perform a perfect breathing technique without thinking about it—they simply do it. We are born with this natural ability to breathe correctly, but we lose it as we grow up. You may think, "I'm perfectly able to breathe!" but the truth is that most of us, led by busy lifestyles, fall into the vice of thoracic breathing. You will have to consciously train your body back to complete breathing, and eventually you will do it naturally.

Breathing completely and correctly calms the mind and spirit, and it makes the body more sensitive and permeable to energies. Traditional Chinese Medicine advises using focused breathing to speed the healing of different illnesses, particularly for those who require calm and need to recover vitality and strength.

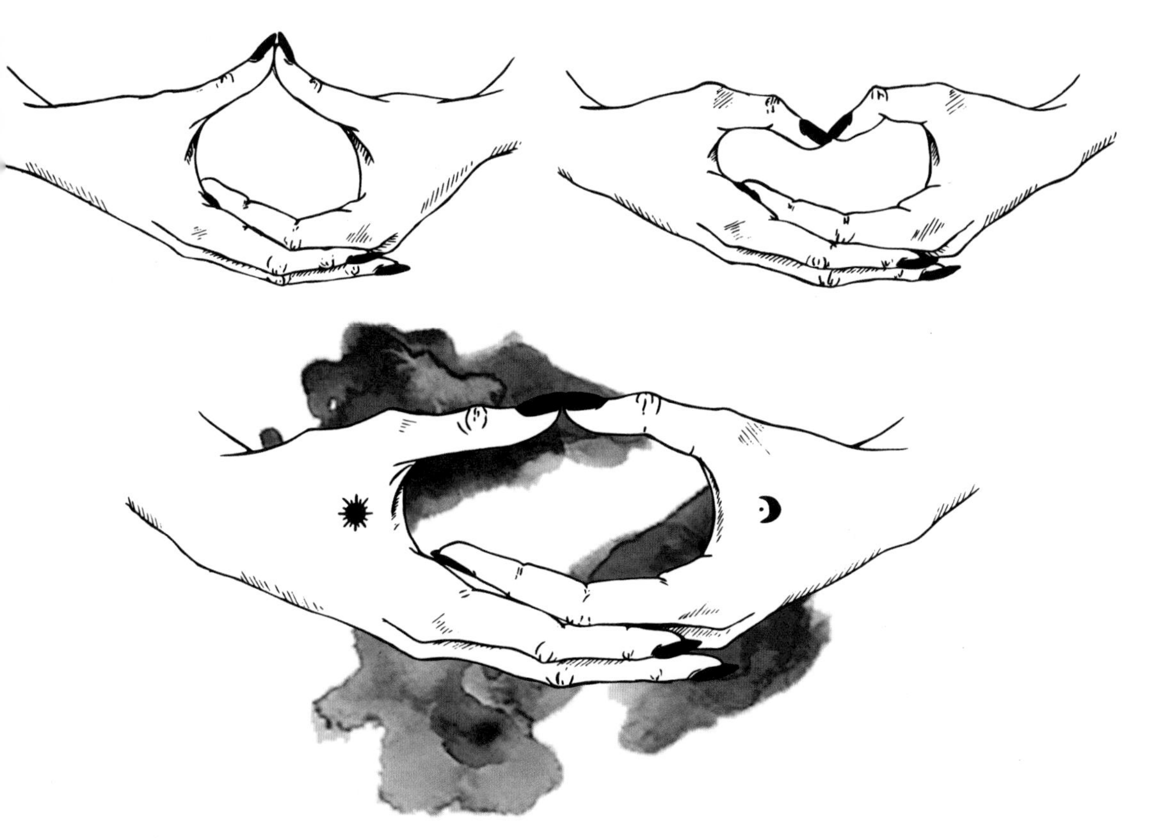

Meditating

Meditating allows you to connect with your true self and enhance your intuition. It teaches you to interact with your feelings and thoughts in a different way. This doesn't mean erasing your feelings. Instead, you acknowledge them without getting tangled up in them. Through awareness, you learn to identify and observe them without judging them.

Sometimes when you are meditating it is difficult to know whether you are in the right mental state: not too relaxed, not too tense. Here is a simple trick that allows you to be conscious of your state: Place your hands on your lap, palm over palm or fingers interlocked, with your thumbs touching their fingertips. Your thumbs should create a straight line. If your thumbs create a V-shape, you are too relaxed. If they create an A-shape, you are too tense.

Getting into the habit of meditating can be hard, but it has so many benefits. Remember: Meditation is a training for your mind and spirit. With regular practice, your abilities will get better over time.

Grounding

Grounding is a form of meditation that allows us to live in the present—to be fully in our body, mind, and the moment. It is used to shake the sensation of being overwhelmed by thoughts or feelings. Grounding links us to the mundane world and to our physical existence, bringing us calm and focus. With this technique we reconnect with Mother Earth and feel centered again.

This exercise works wonders when you are feeling mildly disconnected or when you are struggling. It can even be helpful during an anxiety attack. Simply look around and identify the following, saying each out loud:

- 5 things you can see
- 4 things you can feel
- 3 things you can hear
- 2 things you can smell
- 1 thing you can taste

I have been a highly sensitive person ever since I was young, and this causes me to be easily overwhelmed by certain situations. With time, I have learned that grounding exercises are what work best when I feel disconnected from my body and dissociated from place and time. Doing this exercise helps you regain control over your physical senses, and you will become centered again.

Visualization

Visualization is a process that allows us to create mental images of what we want to generate in the mundane world. Children have a natural capacity for visualizing—usually it is seen as simply daydreaming. Do you remember using your imagination to play, entering fantastic worlds that seemed completely real? That is visualization.

Visualization is essential for focusing the energy that we rise and gather during rituals. It also helps us reconnect with ourselves, allowing us to recognize messages from our intuition more easily. When you visualize, your body and mind become more permeable to the energy that you desire to create. Plus, visualization condenses your intention and helps you project your energy. This way, you boost the results of your work.

When we grow up, we tend to lose the natural ability to visualize. With practice, it can be recovered. Remember: What you visualize doesn't need to be images. Not everybody is a visual person, and some people prefer to guide their inner travels and visualizations with words, sounds, or other sensations.

Intention and Energy Work

In witchcraft, an "intention" is the goal that we establish for a spell or a ritual. In order for it to work, we need to create a slight change in the energy of the universe and orient it toward the fulfillment of our goal. The energy and the network that links everything can't be seen or touched, and we rely on energy work to modify it. Directing and projecting energy can be more or less complex depending on the person. And, as with everything, it can be trained.

First you need to familiarize yourself with your inner energy and how it behaves. With time and practice, you will be able to command it to act as you prefer. Although it takes some people a lot of time to master this, check for energy blockages in your circuit if you are having many problems or if your energy starts to behave in a weird way.

Identifying Your Projective Hand and Your Receptive Hand

We can project and receive energy throughout the body, but there are certain spots or points that are more suitable for energy work. For example, your projecting hand is the one you find easier to use to send energy. Usually this will be your dominant hand, but not always. (I'm right-handed, but my projecting hand is my left hand.) The receptive hand is the one that senses and receives energy.

To identify your projective hand and receptive hand, let your hands rest on your lap and interlock your fingers. Which thumb is on the top of the other? That is your projective hand. To be even more sure you are getting your projective and receptive hand correct, try the exercise in this chapter ("Feel Your Inner Energy" on page 34). Once you can feel the energy flow, it will become clear which hand is sending energy and which one is receiving it.

Keeping all this in mind, when we "charge an object with our intention," we modify its energy with our own. When you focus on your goal and transmit the energy, you will create that subtle change to achieve your goal.

Ethics and Witchcraft

Witchcraft in itself is not linked to any specific ethic or belief system. It is a tool. Many people like to compare it to a knife. Knives were originally conceived of as tools: They have multiple uses; they make our lives easier; they even can be used for self-defense; but, in the hands of the wrong person, a knife can be used to harm people—and if you don't know how to use a knife, you can hurt yourself. This is why knowledge is so important in witchcraft.

Some witches take a vow to not hurt people under any circumstances. For example, the Wiccan rede says: An ye harm none, do what ye will. Other witches guide their acts by the Three-Fold Law, a concept similar to karma. This rule says that the energy that you put into the universe will come back to you multiplied by three. Finally, there are some witches who think that, in the end, how you use your power is up to you and your own ethics.

Personally, I believe that everybody is affected by the Three-Fold Law, so I have chosen to follow the Wiccan rede in my path.

The First Three Steps to Become a Witch

When you feel drawn to the craft, it can seem overwhelming and difficult to know where to begin and to know how magick operates. If you are already initiated, you can skip this section. If you are looking for guidance on how to start walking your path, then this section is perfect for you.

READ A witch is always learning. If you find a book that says something along the lines of "this the only book that you will ever need," don't believe it. It may have complete information about a topic, but it definitely won't be the only one that you will ever need. Be sure to check the reliability of the sources that you consult and double-check the information, particularly with some internet sources.

WRITE One of the best ways to learn and internalize information is to write it down. There are two ways to do so: working on a grimoire or a Book of Shadows (BOS). A grimoire usually only includes information, while a BOS also incorporates a journaling aspect. I usually advise beginner witches to start with a BOS. Keeping a witchcraft journal allows you to learn from your experiences and keep track of your progress.

PRACTICE Knowledge is very important, but it is not everything. If you don't start practicing energy work, psychic skills, and meditation, you won't improve and master them. Start small and gradually add difficulty to your exercises. You will get a better idea of magick and energy after practicing and trying different techniques. Creating a sacred space for your magickal workings will help you with this process. And don't be discouraged if your first spells or rituals don't work. Learn from them. (See "Common Mistakes" in page 167.)

Things I Wish Someone Had Told Me

Stand Up for Yourself

Following the Wiccan rede does not mean letting people hurt you without doing anything about it. It just means not taking the revenge path. You can stand up for yourself, protect yourself, and make others realize that they have done wrong to you. There are also other paths to find a way out of a difficult situation, such as negotiation or ending your relationship.

Try a Chocolate Meditation

Do your meditation attempts usually end in frustration? Then this exercise is for you. Sit in a quiet place and in a comfortable position. Now put an ounce (28 g) of chocolate in your mouth. Explore it with your tongue and feel its shape. Is it square? Rectangular? Are its sides equal or do they have differences? Once it starts to melt, focus on its flavor and smell. Is it sweet or bitter? Does it contain vanilla or other spices? What did you feel when you swallowed the chocolate?

This short exercise combines meditation with mindfulness and grounding, allowing your mind to focus on the activity that you're doing at that moment and freeing it from any other thoughts. Once you have finished your chocolate, you will feel calm and linked to the present moment. The objective of this method is to familiarize yourself with this feeling, so you can reproduce it in other meditation exercises.

Feel Your Inner Energy

Try this static energy work found in qi gong. It combines physical work with breathing and stimulating energy flow.

First, stand with your feet shoulder-width apart and slightly bend your knees. Your spinal column should be straight, but your back should be relaxed, especially at the lumbar region, the level of the dan tian point.

The posture is called "hugging the tree." Spread your arms away from your body and create a circle with them as if you were hugging a big tree. The fingers of one hand should not touch the fingers of the other.

Now, touch the tip of your tongue to the roof of your mouth to close the energy circuit. Start taking complete breaths (see page 26 if you need a reminder about breathing).

Your body may start rocking lightly. Don't worry; this is normal. Concentrate on your movement and reduce it consciously, without tension, until you are static.

Maintain the posture for fifteen to twenty minutes. This takes practice as your body and mind will get tired. Start with just a few minutes and gradually increase the time as you become more comfortable and confident in your practice.

This position allows you to receive a big flow of both yin and yang energy and activates the meridians and natural energy flow of the body. If the exercise is done correctly, you will start feeling your own energy and awakening progressive sensations, such as warmth, tingling, and heaviness. Finally, you will be able to feel the flow in your arms, like a "ball" that goes around the circle that you have created with them.

Once you can feel your energy flow in a steady and constant way, you can practice stopping it. Observe the flow from outside of it, without letting it drag you. It does not need your consciousness to flow, but your will can control it and stop it or project it—with more or less intensity, if needed.

The more familiar you become with your own energy, the easier you will be able to control, project, and use it. The hugging a tree position on its own doesn't allow you to do all of those things, but it helps you feel and focus on your own body and power. This position will allow you to move forward in your practice more quickly and easily than you would without it.

Know When to Rest

Witchcraft is about rituals and spells, learning new things, and working on your magick. Witchcraft is also about resting. Mother Nature rests during winter to blossom in spring, and the moon rests during the new moon to shine again during the full moon. We all need to follow our natural cycle of working and resting.

This can be challenging. I am one of those people who works and practices until I get sick. And even while I am sick, I still feel the need to do things. But the truth is that we need to rest. If you don't listen to the signs that your body and mind give you, you will end up working at 30 percent, but it will feel as if it is 300 percent. You will run the risk of becoming ill.

Give yourself permission to rest and recharge your energy. This is the only way to keep moving forward.

Recharge Yourself: Walk Barefoot Outdoors

If you are feeling tired and dull, it's time to cleanse and recharge yourself. One of the best ways to do this is walking barefoot outside. Make sure that there is nothing dangerous that can hurt your feet.

In the soles of our feet we have an acupuncture point named *yong quan*, which translates as "gushing spring." It is part of the kidney meridian, and it works as a connection between our body and the telluric energy (see "Mother Earth, the Energy of the Universe, and the Five Elements" on page 18). This point serves to recharge our body with the yin energy of the soil, and it also allows us to return toxic energy from our bodies to Mother Earth. This should feel like a bubbling or tingling sensation.

We get yang energy, the energy from the sky, through the *bai hui*, an acupuncture point at the top of our heads. This point matches the crown chakra. The energy should descend through your body, like a fluid. Synchronize your breathing with the energy flow, taking in new energy when you inhale and letting it go when you exhale. Once you learn how to open your doors of the earth and the sky, you will be able to access a higher state of consciousness and be more in tune with Mother Nature and all living beings.

CHAPTER 3

ALTAR AND TOOLS

There are some tools that are strongly linked to witchcraft because they are used to cast spells or perform rituals. They channel and boost energy and intention, but it is through their use that they become sacred and a part of the craft.

The required materials change from one spell or ritual to another. You will see that some items have similar correspondences. My advice is to experiment with different tools and see what fits with your path and tradition. If you feel comfortable using your tools, and if you feel a connection with them, you will be able to grasp all their potential.

This chapter covers the most popular tools that witches use in their rituals and their altars. All these items are sacred once they are incorporated to your Craft, and you will also find why and how to cleanse them and consecrate them. One of the things I love about witchcraft is that tools are sacred, but they are made to be used, and that's why I've incorporate several practical approaches like how to create your own portable altar or how to find/make your own inexpensive supplies.

The Altar

Your altar is a sacred place designated for your magick workings. This means an altar is a workplace, not just a decoration. It doesn't need to be big or fancy; it has to be personal and useful. At your altar you should place the items that you need for your craft.

Before setting up your altar, it is important to cleanse the space to dispel any unwanted energies that can affect the proceedings or outcome of your rituals or spells. (For details, see chapter 9 on page 141.) Once you have arranged all your items, it is time to bless your altar. There are many different ways to bless an altar. Perform the blessing that fits your beliefs.

Tools

ALTAR PLATES From actual plates to crystal slabs or engraved wood pieces, altar plates are used to display items, make offerings, or simply decorate your altar. Some designs allow them to be used as crystal grids (see "Crystal Grids" on page 86) or to consecrate pentacles.

ATHAME An athame is a ceremonial knife used for energy work. Creating an athame usually involves four elements: fire, water, air, and earth. Traditionally, it has a double-edged blade and a black handle. Its shape makes it perfect to channel energy. Athames are personal and should be used only by the owner. Your athame is sacred and should only be used for your craft.

BOLINE A boline is a ritual knife used for cutting and carving. A boline usually has a white handle, one edge, and a crescent-shaped blade. However, you can find them with a straight blade. Like athames, bolines are sacred, and it is advised to use them only for your craft.

BOOK OF SHADOWS (BOS) OR GRIMOIRE A BOS and a grimoire are both sacred books that help witches on their path. They are very personal because they contain spells, rituals, and the knowledge necessary to put them into practice. A BOS is also part journal. In it, you can pour out your personal thoughts and experiences regarding your craft.

BROOMS In pop culture representations, broomsticks are one of the items with the strongest connection to witches. Brooms have, in fact, a strong relationship with witchcraft. They are used to sweep away negative energies and protect houses from evil. They represent the union of femininity (the brush) and masculinity (the handle). They are also used in some Wiccan handfasting rituals (pagan weddings). The belief that brooms are used to fly comes from the Middle Ages. Some witches made anointments with hallucinogenic plants that were applied to the mucous membranes and other body parts. Witches anointed their brooms with the ointments and then rode the brooms naked, giving them the feeling of "flying."

CANDLES Candle magick is deeply rooted in many cultures, not only in the ones related to witchcraft. For example, making a wish while blowing out birthday candles is a form of candle magick. Candles are linked to the element fire, representing change, transformation, determination, and action. Because of this, they are a very common element in many spells and rituals. Different colored candles are used depending on the goal of the spell. (See "Colors" on page 142.)

CAULDRON Cauldrons have many uses in witchcraft, from making potions to burning herbs. In modern witchcraft, small-size iron cauldrons are commonly used to burn herbs (see "My Favorite Herb Blend for Regular Cleansing" on page 99). If you don't have a cauldron, you can also use a fireproof cooking pot.

CHALICE There is no better way to represent the element of water on an altar than with a chalice. This water is blessed and used in purifying rituals. Some group rituals incorporate wine that is drunk by all the participants from the same chalice to represent the unity among all the members. Due to their shape, chalices are also a strong tool for fertility rituals.

DEITIES' REPRESENTATIONS Witches who work with deities may keep a physical representation of them on the altar. Representations allow deities to channel their presence into the mundane world and lend us their energy, as well as receive offerings. Not all deities or traditions require a physical representation. Deities can be portrayed with figurines, paintings, animal parts, herbs, objects, and many other items, as each deity has its own correspondences.

HERBS Herbs have correspondences that have been assigned to them through years of witchcraft practice. Although they are used extensively in green and kitchen witchcraft, they have many magickal and medicinal properties that any witch may find useful. They can be burned, incorporated into recipes, placed in pouches, and put to many other uses. (See chapter 6 to learn more about herbs.)

INCENSE Different scents have been used since ancient times to create a change in the conscious and subconscious minds. With its smoke, incense dispels negative energies, blesses the space, and carries our messages to deities or the universe.

JARS They are the best friend of green witches, as jars allow us to preserve many herbs, tinctures, and other concoctions in an eco-friendly way. Jars are also used in different spells to concentrate their energy. Spell jars are usually sealed with wax.

MIRRORS Reflective surfaces have a strong presence in witchcraft. They are used in protection spells as a way to reverse (reflect) the negative energy that comes at you. They are also considered portals to other realms. Treat them as windows and trace invisible sigils on them to keep them closed. If you have a mirror in your bedroom, avoid having it facing your bed while you are asleep.

MORTAR AND PESTLE This is a handy tool, especially when working with herbs. They are usually made from stone or wood, and they help us create the perfect blend of herbs, spices, and other dry goods. Some people like to add oil to create oil blends, but this can make the mortar and pestle more difficult to clean.

OIL BLENDS Oil blends are mixes of different oils, herbs, and spices. They are traditionally used to anoint candles and other tools, and the ingredients and their use are deeply interconnected. For example, if we want to create an oil blend for protection, we use olive oil as a carrier oil and add clove oil, rosemary oil, and a cinnamon stick. These herbs are some of the most powerful ones for protection, plus they will give a nice smell to the candle. (Powdered cinnamon is flammable, so it is better to just use a cinnamon stick.)

PENTACLE A pentacle is an upright five-pointed star with a circle around it. Each point of the star represents one of the five elements, and the circle around it symbolizes that the five elements make a whole. Pentacles are used to represent the elements in rituals, but they also have inherent powers. They are used as strong protection symbols, and some blessing rituals include laying the item on an altar plate with a pentacle engraved on it. I always wear a small silver pentacle necklace.

SALT This mineral is very important in many forms of witchcraft. It is used to absorb negative energies from the environment, creating a "clean bubble" around your altar. Salt is also incorporated into spells as a protection source. All types of salt are used to guard from negative energies, and each type has different nuances and properties.

WAND Wands, like athames, are a personal tool used to channel your energy. They usually measure the length from your elbow to the tip of your index finger. Traditionally, wands are made from willow, oak, apple, or cherry wood. If you find a branch that you feel drawn to, you can use it as well. Some witches like to have different wands from different woods and use them depending on the intention of their spell. Drawing down the moon is one of the most popular rituals that incorporates the use of a wand.

WATER Water is used to represent its element on your altar. It is also a powerful cleansing tool, and when blessed it can be used to consecrate other tools as well. Waters from different sources have different correspondences. (See "Moon Water" on page 159, to learn more about the significance of moon water.)

Consecrating Tools

Many pagan traditions cleanse, consecrate, and charge their tools before using them, but there are some that don't. My personal advice is to do it. By following these rituals you eliminate any unwanted energies from your magickal tools, and you prepare them to work with the energy of the Divine and the universe.

It is important to follow the correct order when cleansing, consecrating, and charging to avoid attaching mixed or unwanted energies to your magickal tools.

Cleansing is basically using energy to clean something. By cleansing new objects, you protect yourself from any unwanted energy that may be attached to the object. Through a ritual, you disturb the energy attached to an object (or a person) and cut its link to them (see "Cleansing" on page 156). Old energies are not necessarily bad energies, but their vibrations can alter the outcome of your rituals and spells. Think of it like if you write on a sheet of paper that is already written on. The old letters would interfere with the new ones, making it confusing and affecting the message and the final result. You need to erase all the existing content before creating your own.

Consecrating consists of blessing your tools to transform everyday items into sacred tools suitable for magickal practices. Consecrated items should be treated as such and can't be used again in mundane workings.

Charging your tools is imbuing them with the energy that you want them to hold. This energy can vary depending on the ritual that you want to perform, ranging from your personal energy to the energy of the full moon and many others (see "Charging" on page 158).

You can cleanse and charge your items (and yourself) whenever you need to. If you feel that something is off with one of your tools, it may be time to repeat these actions. My advice is to include cleansing and charging your tools as a part of all of your important rituals and spells.

Things I Wish Someone Had Told Me

Create a Portable Altar

If you are like me and are always traveling, or if you prefer to keep your craft discreet, a portable altar is a great option. You can create one in a small box and include the tools that are essential for your craft as well as an altar cloth. When needed, cleanse a space, set out your altar cloth, and arrange the items. Bless your altar and you are ready to go. Once you have finished your spell, ritual, offering, or prayer, give thanks to the universe or your deities and place everything inside the box again!

Here are some items to incorporate into your portable altar:

- Small birthday candles in a range of colors
- Mini bottles with premade herbal blends
- Matches
- Representations of your deities (You can paint them inside the lid of the box.)
- A small piece of clear quartz or other crystal
- A pentacle to represent the five elements
- Salt
- One or two incense cones
- A small plate to hold the candles and burn the cones safely

Modify it as much as you want! Always keep in mind that it has to be useful and small, so include only what is indispensable. If you are on a trip, calculate how many days you will be away from your altar and only include supplies for those days (and maybe one more for emergencies).

Salt Sourcing

Because of its properties, salt is one of the most popular elements with witches. It is usually a must-have in every witch kit. However, its sourcing may affect and disrupt its energy. Get your salt from ethical sources that are responsible toward the environment. Also, sea salt may not be the best choice because of its high microplastic content; more than 90 percent of table salt sourced from the sea contains microplastics.

Magickal Substitutions

The only ingredient that is essential in all spells and rituals is your intention. All the rest of the items used in magickal workings are aimed to boost your intention. Some ingredients match one type of intention better than others. (See "Correspondences" on page 142, for more about correspondences.)

Sometimes when we want to cast a spell, we realize that we don't have all the necessary ingredients. This is when all-purpose items come in handy.

ITEM	HOW TO SUBSTITUTE IT
Colored candles	White candles with your intention carved in them
Crystals	Clear quartz programmed (see "Clear Quartz, page 78) with your intention
Herbs	Rosemary
Poisonous herbs	Tobacco
Flowers	Roses
Fruits	Apples
Citrus	Lemons
Gum resin	Frankincense
Teas	Black tea

My advice is not to substitute more than one item per spell. These substitutions are only adequate for magickal workings. If you need the chemical or medicinal properties of an item, do not substitute it. For example, if you want to make calendula salve for dry hands, you can't substitute roses for calendula.

Finding Inexpensive Supplies

Sometimes people have the idea that it is expensive to be a witch. That could not be further from the truth! When you decide to start walking the witchcraft path, most of the items that you need can be found for little to no money. You can also save a bit by making them yourself. Be creative and think about how you could use something for your craft when you encounter it.

Here are ideas for inexpensive or DIY supplies:

- Buy candles from home décor shops.
- Birthday candles can be used for some rituals (and they take less time to burn completely if you need it to be quick).
- Make altar cloths from old T-shirts.
- Seasonal home décor items can be used as altar décor to match each sabbat. (See chapter 4.)
- Use things that you find in nature, such as leaves or stones. Make sure not to harm the environment by picking them.
- Seeds are cheaper than plants. Grow your own herbs in pots or in your garden. (See chapter 6.)

Be imaginative! I'm always checking markets and bazaars trying to find things that I can incorporate into my altar or a tool that will allow me to craft something new.

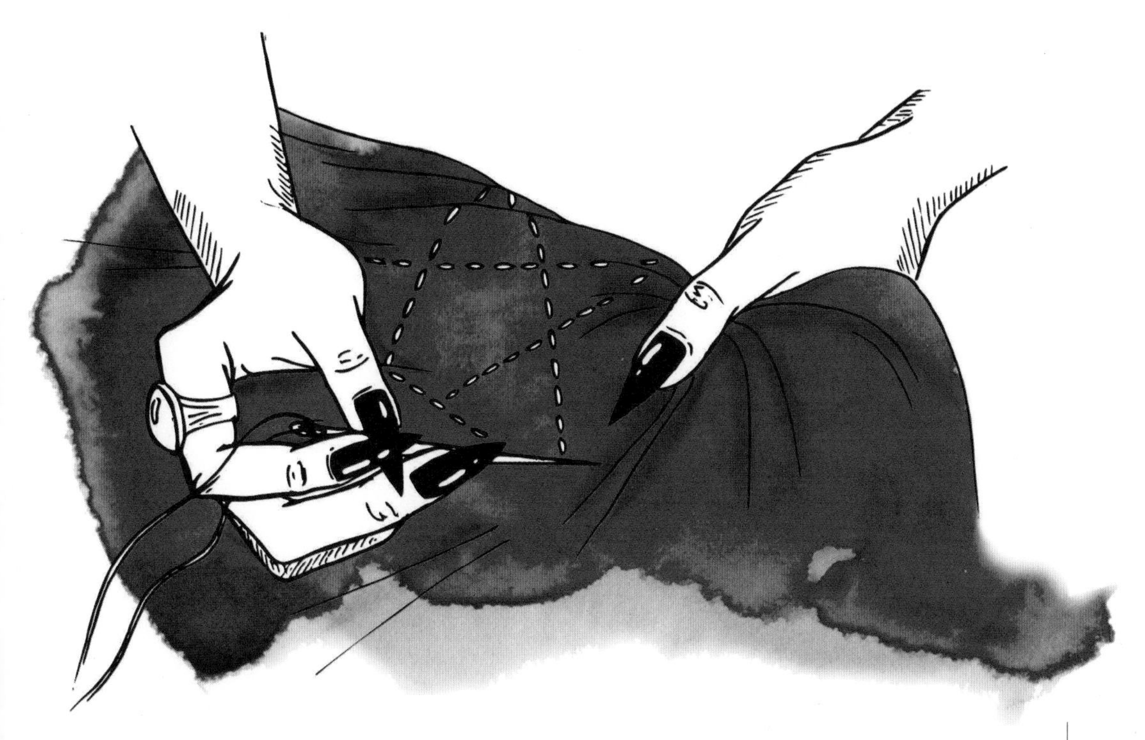

CHAPTER 4

The Wheel of the Year

Ever since ancient times, the cycles of nature have been celebrated with rituals and festivals. The Wheel of the Year is drawn from Wiccan and pagan practice. It consists of eight holidays, or sabbats, that mark the change of seasons and nature's cycles. Many witches celebrate these holidays as a way to feel more connected to Mother Earth.

The eight holidays are the spokes of the Wheel of the Year, and they are days of high energy and symbolism. All of the sabbats are joyfully celebrated with music, dancing, and feasting. Some pagans like to visit Stonehenge or other significant places that were oriented to celebrate a sabbat with the sunrise or sunset.

The Wheel of the Year is divided into four Greater Sabbats and four Lesser Sabbats. This designation is based on their origin and the astronomical event that they celebrate.

The Greater Sabbats occur on dates of high energy related to the different stages of the harvest: resting, planting, sprouting, and harvesting. The day of the peak power of each season is chosen to celebrate these sabbats. They are also named the Earth Festivals because of their relationship with natural cycles. Every year, Mother Nature wakes up from the winter sleep, bringing new leaves and flowers with her that will give fruit and be harvested just before she goes to sleep once again. This cycle is repeated every year. If we imagine the year as a wheel, these sabbats are positioned in the four cardinal points. This is what gives them the name of the cross-quarter days. They trace their roots to the Celtic Fire Festivals that were celebrated before the rise of Christianity. They are always celebrated on the same day.

The Lesser Sabbats celebrate the change of seasons. They are also called the Sun Festivals because they fall on the equinoxes and solstices. This causes the dates to vary slightly when they are celebrated from one year to another, as the solstice and equinox astronomical dates change.

This close relationship between nature's cycles and astronomical events generates two different

Wheels of the Year: one for the northern hemisphere and one for the southern hemisphere. They celebrate the opposite sabbat on the same day because the two hemispheres experience opposite seasons. This is caused by the tilt of the Earth on its axis, causing one hemisphere to be more exposed to the sun's rays. When the northern hemisphere faces the sun, experiencing summer, the southern hemisphere is less exposed to the sunlight, experiencing winter, and vice versa.

As all the sabbats originate from ancient European traditions, their celebrations and practices reflect those old customs. You can see some examples of this in the worship of the sun and life in Yule with candles and evergreens or in the rituals that involve preserving food during Lughnasadh, Mabon, and Samhain.

SABBAT	SABBAT TYPE	EVENT	NORTHERN HEMISPHERE	SOUTHERN HEMISPHERE
Yule	Lesser Sabbat	Winter Solstice	December 20–23	June 20–23
Imbolc	Greater Sabbat	First Fire Festival	February 1	August 1
Ostara	Lesser Sabbat	Spring Equinox	March 20–23	September 20–23
Beltane	Greater Sabbat	Second Fire Festival	May 1	October 31
Litha	Lesser Sabbat	Summer Solstice	June 20–23	December 20–23
Lughnasadh	Greater Sabbat	Third Fire Festival	August 1	February 1
Mabon	Lesser Sabbat	Autumn Equinox	September 20–23	March 20–23
Samhain	Greater Sabbat	Fourth Fire Festival	October 31	May 1

Yule

Yule is celebrated on the winter equinox, the shortest day of the year. During this time, the coldest days are approaching, but sunlight will soon start canceling out the darkness as the days grow incrementally longer. Yule represents the paradox of the death and rebirth of the sun.

Nothing grows in the fields, and the land seems to be barren. Evergreens acquire particular importance, as they remind us that life is still out there beneath the frozen ground and it will return in spring. Yule is a quiet reminder of the renewal of life. Cold, dark days call us to be introspective, seek the company of our loved ones, light a fire, and decorate the hearth. Yule reminds us to cherish what we have and share it with those dearest to us.

The origin of the word *yule* isn't clear, as it has been adopted and modified by several languages. One of the most accepted beliefs is that it derives from the Old Norse word *hjól*, which means "wheel," referring to the Wheel of the Year that starts to spin once again. If we understand the year as a series of sabbats on a wheel, celebrating Yule means that a cycle has been completed, thus a new cycle starts. Another version says that *yule* comes from the Old English word *yoole*, which once again derives from Old Norse, but this time from *jól*, a term used in the descriptions and names of the Norse gods as well as a synonym for "feast."

Many different traditions throughout Europe celebrated this moment of the year, from the Germanic and Celtic pagans to the festival of Saturnalia in ancient Rome. Many of the activities and decorations related to this sabbat (and even the date) were appropriated by the Christian church in an attempt to erase Yule when Christianity became the mandatory religion in the Roman Empire. You will see that many Christmas traditions are similar to those of Yule, but, as most historians agree, Christ wasn't born during winter. This pattern of appropriating pagan festivities and traditions repeats itself in other sabbats and time periods, as it was a common way to promote and establish the Christian religion while gaining more followers.

Yule Correspondences

COLORS Green, red, and gold are the colors of this sabbat, as they represent nature, the sun, and the return of longer, warmer days.

EVERGREEN PLANTS Evergreens represent the everlasting quality of life. Even if we can't see crops in the fields or leaves on the branches, the life force still exists, sleeping and waiting for spring to come. Some examples of evergreen plants are pine cones to promote joy in your home, mistletoe for protection, and ivy as a symbol of immortality.

CANDLES Candles are also an important part of Yule traditions, as they bring light and warmth into the darkness. They are most often used in the traditional green, red, and gold colors, sometimes with a touch of shimmer or glitter to make them shinier. In modern times, candles have been substituted in some instances by strings of lights.

MAGICK The wheel starts a new cycle, and so do we. The dark, long winter afternoons are a perfect time to meditate and reflect on our lives. The Earth is resting, and so are we. This is a perfect moment to start thinking about new projects, setting your intentions for the year ahead, and renewing your hopes.

FOOD When this festival was established, fresh fruits and vegetables weren't available during winter. Because of this, most of the food consumed during this sabbat was meat, some grains, dried fruits, wine, and any preserved foods that were stored during the harvest.

Yule Activities

DECORATE A YULE TREE The Yule tree is an evergreen tree growing outdoors, not cut down and taken inside. It is decorated with candles and other ornaments that symbolize the return of the sun. Other traditional decorations are garlands of dried fruits, a representation of the presents that we want to receive from Mother Earth. The Yule tree is usually linked to the Tree of Life: the connection between the sky and the earth, a symbol of immortality, and the links between all the elements of the universe.

BURN A YULE LOG This tradition originated in Scandinavia, where the Yule log represents the Green Man, the god that symbolizes the spirit of nature, which was cut down during the last harvest and will grow again in spring. You can use any type of wood, but traditionally the Yule log is made from oak, birch, or fruit trees. The Yule log is decorated with candles and evergreens and then blessed. Oftentimes it is used as a centerpiece during the Yule dinner. Afterward, a ceremony is held where the five elements (air, fire, water, earth, and spirit) and Mother Nature are thanked. Then the Yule log is burned in the fireplace. Don't let it burn completely; save a part of the log to kindle next Yule's fire. Spread the ashes from the fire back into the earth.

HANG MISTLETOE This plant was sacred to the Druids. It was collected during the winter solstice and hung in the home to promote fertility and peace.

EXCHANGE GIFTS Yule is strongly related to gift giving. Winter was a hard time for those who had less, and Yule provided a means to help others survive the winter. This custom also extended to giving presents to family and friends to show affection.

HANG WREATHS Made with evergreens, pine cones, and berries, wreaths remind us that another cycle has been completed. They were hung on the front door to protect a home from evil spirits and illness. They were also given as a present to celebrate love and friendship.

PREPARE A FEAST Feasting is an important aspect of every sabbat. However, it is particularly significant during Yule, as it celebrates the fact that the Earth will yield her fruits once again during the next harvest.

Yule Recipe: Winter Harvest Purée

The cold winter days call for a warm purée. This recipe will give you a boost of energy, and most of its ingredients can be stored during winter.

Yield: 6 servings

2 pounds (1 kg) potatoes, peeled
1 pound (½ kg) pumpkin, peeled and seeded
1 carrot
2 onions
1 leek
1 cup (235 ml) cream
1½ tablespoons (20 g) butter
Pinch each of salt, pepper, and nutmeg

Dice the potatoes, pumpkin, carrot, onions, and leek. Put them in a pot, cover them with water, and boil them until soft. Strain off the vegetable stock and set aside. Add the cream, butter, salt, pepper, and nutmeg to the vegetables. Mash them until everything is well incorporated. Serve hot. If the texture of the purée is too thick, add some of the vegetable stock until it has your desired consistency.

Imbolc

Imbolc, the first fire festival, celebrates winter transforming into spring. The sun is slowly but steadily coming back, adding a few extra minutes of light each day. Slowly the ice and snow are starting to melt. These first sunbeams and drops of water are waking Mother Nature from her long slumber. The return of spring is imminent. Imbolc is a time for healing and rebirth.

Although the Wiccan tradition celebrates it on February 1, the festival can extend from January 31 to February 2.

The sabbat emphasizes milk, as the time of year is associated with the traditional lambing season. Imbolc is also named *Oimelc*, which means "ewe's milk." *Imbolc* means "in the belly," referring to the pregnancy of ewes and cows. As the last provisions from the harvest were running out, milk made it possible for the ancient Celts to survive the end of the winter.

This sabbat is sacred to the Celtic triple goddess, Brigid. Her name means "the exalted one" and she is the bringer of civilization, spring, healing, and fertility. She is the patroness of smithcraft and poetry. She is commonly represented along with her two sisters, to emphasize her triple aspect. Christians assimilated some elements of Brigid the goddess into Saint Brigid.

Imbolc Correspondences

COLORS White and red are the colors for this sabbat. White represents the melting snow and the milk from the ewes. Red symbolizes the sun and fire that are celebrated during Imbolc.

CANDLES Imbolc is one of the fire festivals, and flames are always present. They are a reminder of the growing strength of the sun.

BRIGID CROSS This ancient symbol sacred to the goddess Brigid consists of weaving rushes or straws to create a squared pattern. They were placed in homes for protection, especially against house fires.

MAGICK This sabbat is especially favorable for magick that involves getting rid of what no longer serves you. If you need to improve your psychic skills, practice different types of divination during this sabbat to get more precise answers.

FOOD Milk and other dairy products are strongly related to Imbolc. Milk was available only while cows, sheep, and goats were nursing their young. Imbolc was a time to make cheese and other dairy products to store them during the rest of the year. Representations of sheep, cows, and goats were also common during this time of the year. Nowadays, some pagans substitute animal milk with plant milk.

Imbolc Activities

CLEAN AND TIDY YOUR HOUSE
Imbolc cleansing is the neo-pagan version of spring cleaning. Cleaning your home and getting rid of what is no longer needed is a perfect way to prepare to receive the blessing of the upcoming year. In addition, you can use this as an opportunity to cleanse your house of unwanted energies. (See chapter 9 on page 141.)

PRACTICE DIVINATION Imbolc is a good moment to practice divination; in particular, try fire scrying or water scrying using melted snow. (See chapter 7 on page 107.)

LIGHT CANDLES Light one candle in each room of your home after sunset to honor the death and rebirth of the sun.

VISIT A RIVER Go to a nearby river or spring and let the flowing waters cleanse you as Mother Nature imbues and invigorates you with her sacred energy.

CREATE TALISMANS Imbolc is the optimal time to create talismans that you will carry or place in your house for the rest of the year. One of the most common talismans of Imbolc is the Brigid Cross.

MAKE CHEESE Imbolc is related to canning and preserving food, especially milk. It provides us the opportunity to connect with our ancestors by making some traditional cheese, yogurt, or butter recipes.

Imbolc Recipe: Kefir

One of my favorite Imbolc activities is making kefir. Kefir is a drink made from milk, and it is similar to yogurt. It originated in the Caucasus and is traditionally made with sheep or goat milk; however, cow milk works well too. Seeds are strongly related to Imbolc, as spring is returning and it is time to plant them. I chose to add poppy seeds here because poppy seed cake is a traditional Imbolc recipe.

Yield: 3 cups (710 ml) of kefir

2 tablespoons (30 g) kefir seeds
3 cups (710 ml) whole goat milk
Sugar or honey (optional)
Poppy seeds (optional)

Place the kefir seeds and the milk in a clean glass jar. It should be two-thirds full to leave room for air so the kefir can breathe. Close the jar and leave it at room temperature to ferment for about 8 hours.

Strain the mixture to separate the kefir from the milk and drink it! If it is too sour, you can add some sugar or honey. Add poppy seeds for an extra Imbolc touch. Rinse the kefir seeds with warm water and they are ready to be used again.

Ostara

Ostara is the first day of spring. It's a date of perfect balance, as day and night split the day in two equal periods of twelve hours. It is a time to reflect on the duality of life, as light and darkness, life and death, are always in balance.

Mother Nature is waking up from her death sleep and we start seeing signs of her return. Snow has melted and life is sprouting up through the earth. Ostara is the season of fertility, a celebration of life's ability to rise from the ashes.

You will see some similarities with the celebrations of this sabbat and the Anglo-Saxon and North American Easter, starting with its name. The origin of the name Ostara comes from Eostre, the Germanic goddess of spring.

Ostara Correspondences

COLORS Pastel colors are the most common colors for this sabbat. They represent the tender spring shoots that are starting to grow.

EGGS Eggs represent the potential of life and the rebirth of Mother Nature. The round shape links them to the cycle of life, and the golden yolk links them to the coming summer sun.

HARE This animal is strongly related to Ostara due to its fertility. Sometimes hares are also linked to the cycles of the moon and women. Rabbits and hares have been related to the goddess Eostre as well.

MAGICK This sabbat is very favorable for self-improvement rituals and new beginnings. If you want to start a new project, this is the perfect moment to do so. Remember to ground yourself before starting new journeys.

FOOD This sabbat is especially related to baking. One of the most traditional recipes is baking hot cross buns, a type of spiced sweet bun marked with a cross on top. Chocolate rabbits are also eaten during this sabbat.

Ostara Activities

PRACTICE SEED MAGICK Seeds symbolize the upcoming spring, the awakening of Mother Nature after the winter. Plan your garden and start some seeds inside. You can put your intention in the seeds, so it grows as the plants grow.

DECORATE EGGS Use natural dyes to paint your eggs. Decorate them with pagan symbols and drawings to represent spring. Eggshells make great containers to start seeds: once the plant has grown, you only need to crack the eggshell a bit and you can plant it directly in the soil.

REPRESENT BALANCE THROUGH YOUR SURROUNDINGS You can add decorations to your house that represent the balance between day and night. Use images of the sun and moon or burn a black candle and a white candle.

GIVE GIFTS OF POTTED PLANTS Give plants to your friends and family to wish them a prosperous year.

CREATE A RITUAL ROBE Design and create an outfit to wear during the celebration of Ostara.

Ostara Recipe: Hot Cross Buns

Apart from being a traditional Ostara recipe, hot cross buns are mouthwatering! This recipe is not the easiest one in this book, but it is completely worth the effort.

Yield: 12 to 15 buns

Buns

2 tablespoons (20 g) active dry yeast
1 tablespoon (15 ml) lukewarm water
3½ cups (500 g) all-purpose flour
¼ cup (50 g) sugar
1 teaspoon ground cinnamon
½ teaspoon ground nutmeg
1 cup (235 ml) milk
2 eggs, divided (set aside 1 yolk)
¼ cup (50 g) butter, melted
½ teaspoon vanilla extract
Zest from 1 orange
¾ cup (100 g) seedless raisins

Cross

½ cup (100 g) sugar
½ cup (120 ml) milk

Preheat the oven to 375ºF (190ºC, or gas mark 5) and grease a baking sheet.

To make the buns: Place the yeast in a small bowl and add the lukewarm water; set aside to proof. In a large bowl, combine the flour, sugar, cinnamon, and nutmeg. In a separate large bowl, combine the yeast, milk, 2 egg whites and 1 egg yolk, melted butter, vanilla, and orange zest. Pour the wet ingredients over the dry ingredients and add the raisins. Mix well to form a dough. Turn out onto a lightly floured surface and knead for 10 minutes.

Shape into 12 to 15 balls and place them on the greased pan. Cover with a damp cloth and let them rise for 1 to 2 hours until they double in size.

Whisk the remaining egg yolk in a small bowl and paint the surface of the dough balls. Bake the buns for 20 minutes.

To make the cross: Mix the sugar with the milk in a bowl. Fill a piping bag and paint a cross on each bun.

Beltane

The second fire festival celebrates the middle of spring. We can appreciate life and nature in all its splendor. Trees have recovered all their leaves and the fields are full of flowers. Beltane is the sabbat that marks the starting date of outdoor festivals as the weather is more pleasant.

Beltane strongly celebrates love, sexuality, and fertility. It is a date that many pagans choose for handfasting (pagan weddings). Beltane may come from the Celtic god Belenus, who was the god of the sun and commonly associated with a horse and a wheel. Beltane is strongly associated with the sun, and this also reminds us of the god Helios, who flew across the sky in a horse-drawn chariot. What we see of him from Earth is the halo of his shiny crown—the sun.

Beltane Correspondences

COLORS The predominant colors are green, yellow, red, and lilac. These represent the leaves that now cover the trees and the flowers that are blooming.

FIRE This fire festival is celebrated with bonfires. These fires are both a representation of the sun and a sacred offering to the sun.

RIBBONS Ribbons are used in several important rituals, such as the Maypole dance, dressing a tree, and handfasting. They are deeply related to this sabbat. Their bright colors remind us of flowers, and when knotted, ribbons are a representation of love.

FLOWERS Everything is blooming. The colors and scents of flowers flood the atmosphere. They are the sign that nature will bear fruit. Flowers are usually linked to the bees that pollinate them, allowing them to produce seeds for new generations.

FAERIES This sabbat is said to be a day of special connection between our world and the spirit realm. During Beltane, faeries are particularly active and are more noticeable. It is traditional to leave them some offerings such as milk with honey.

MAGICK Beltane is favorable for all types of love magick and fertility magick.

FOOD Celebrate Beltane with all types of early vegetables and fruits, such as cherries or strawberries. To give a more colorful look to your dishes, you can also add edible flowers.

Beltane Activities

DANCE AROUND A MAYPOLE A Maypole is a tall pole decorated with leaves and flowers. Ribbons are tied to the top part of the pole and the dancers weave them around it while they perform the dance. This ritual promotes the fertility of the earth.

DRESS A TREE Chose a birch or a rowan to decorate with flowers, wreaths, and ribbons with wishes and blessings written on them. You can choose another type of tree if you have a special connection with it. Once you have finished the ritual, gather everything that you brought. Say a blessing over them and return anything natural to Mother Earth. (Keep any elements that aren't biodegradable for next year's festival.)

WEAR A FLOWER CROWN People wear flower crowns during Beltane to celebrate the spring. They are also used to decorate homes and the Maypole. Sometimes this type of wreath is also decorated with ribbons.

CHOOSE A MAY QUEEN AND A GREEN MAN They are usually drawn by lot. The May Queen represents the purity and energy of nature, and the Green Man represents the life that is sprouting.

HANDFASTING This ceremony is the pagan version of a wedding. Depending on the tradition that you follow, the ceremony may include rituals such as wrapping the hands of the couple with a ribbon or the couple jumping the broom. The strong relationship of Beltane with love and fertility makes it one of the most popular dates to celebrate this ceremony.

Beltane Recipe: Candied Flowers

Bring the beauty of blossoms to your kitchen. Flowers have a wide range of flavors, from sweet to sour or even spicy. This recipe for candied flowers has roots in the Victorian era, and they make excellent natural sweets or decorations. Caution: Not all flowers are edible. Be sure to do your research before eating them.

Yield: 1 to 2 cups (50 to 100 g) of candied flowers

- 1 egg white, pasteurized
- 1 cup (235 ml) water
- 1 cup (about 45 g) small edible flowers or 2 cups (about 80 g) large edible flowers (I like to use rose petals and pansies.)
- ½ cup (100 g) caster sugar

The process is pretty simple. In a small bowl, whisk the egg white to break the albumin and then mix it with the water. Try not to make many bubbles.

Use a brush to paint the flowers with the mixture or dip them in it directly. Then, cover them completely with the caster sugar. Leave them to dry on wax paper undisturbed for 24 hours.

I like to use candied flowers to decorate cakes or fruit salads. If you keep them in an airtight jar in a cold, dark place, they can last for up to a year.

Litha

The longest day of the year is an event that celebrates the triumph of nature, embodied as the Green Man or the Oak King. The warm sunlight filters between the green leaves of trees. It is the peak of the light, but it is also the beginning of its decline.

Litha is usually celebrated outdoors. The warmth and light of the sun blesses us as it blessed the crops in the fields. It is the ideal period to celebrate fairs and other festivities. Litha shares some similarities with Beltane, especially their relationship with faeries and fire. In some places, Litha is also called Midsummer or takes the Christian name Saint John's Eve.

Litha Correspondences

COLORS All of the warm colors from yellow to red are present to call to mind the warmth of summer. Blue and green are also prominent during Litha to represent the sky and green leaves.

FIRE To accompany and strengthen the sun on its journey, this sabbat was celebrated by lighting torches and bonfires and incorporating them into rituals. To maintain the balance of the universe, the element water is usually a part of the celebrations as well.

HERBS Most herbs used in witchcraft and traditional medicine are ready to be harvested. Long, hot days are the perfect time to dry them and store them.

FAERIES At this time of the year, faeries are even more active than during Beltane. Some witches choose this date to invoke them and win their favor. Keep in mind that faeries are volatile, and they may choose to trick you instead of helping you.

MAGICK Litha is favorable for all kinds of sun magick, as well as reaffirming the goals that you have set during Yule.

FOOD Summer berries and honey are ready to be harvested. The land is producing vegetables and fruits. It is a perfect time to bake fruit cakes or honey cakes.

Litha Activities

LOOK FOR HAGSTONES Also called adder stones, hagstones have naturally occurring holes. They are usually found near water. It is said that if you look through the hole you will be able to see the realm of the faeries.

BURN THE PAST Think about the situations in your life that need closure or something that you want to leave behind. Write it on a piece of paper and burn it in Lithia's bonfires before the bonfire leaping ritual.

LEAP THE BONFIRE Lighting a bonfire and jumping over it is a traditional way to ask Mother Nature for her blessings. Usually, you set an intention for this year and seal it by jumping. Always be careful when using fire in your rituals.

PLAY AND ENJOY MUSIC It is said that faeries love music, and playing it is a way to keep them happy. If you celebrate Litha during the night, the sunset and sunrise are usually celebrated with percussion to encourage the sun on its journey.

SET A WHEEL ON FIRE This ritual is very symbolic: A wheel was set on fire to represent the sun, then it was thrown downhill while burning. As the wheel rolled down the hill, it embodied the idea of the days starting to get shorter. It landed in a body of water. This ritual can be dangerous, as it can start a wildfire.

Litha Recipe: Honey Cakes

This version of honey cakes is one of my favorite breakfasts, particularly if accompanied with fresh fruit. Delicious!

Yield: 4 to 6 cakes

1 cup (125 g) flour
1 tablespoon (14 g) baking powder
¾ cup (180 ml) milk, plus more if needed
2 tablespoons (30 ml) olive oil, preferably extra-virgin
1 egg
Honey, to taste
Butter or oil, for frying

In a bowl, mix the flour and baking powder, then add the milk, olive oil, egg, and honey (to your taste). Stir until smooth. If the batter is very thick, add a bit more milk.

Heat a medium pan and grease it with butter or oil. Pour some batter into the pan and let it cook until bubbles start appearing on the surface. Flip it and let it cook on the other side. Serve the honey cakes with a bit more honey, if you prefer.

Lughnasadh

The season of the harvest is upon us. The sun is at its zenith, and we celebrate the middle of the summer. From now on, the days will be shorter until they find their perfect balance again on the autumnal equinox.

Lughnasadh is the first of the three harvests of the Wheel of the Year, and it's the third fire festival. The harvest was a moment of great celebration and happiness, as the survival of ancient European inhabitants during winter depended on it. A good harvest means abundance for the rest of the year. Lughnasadh invites us to reflect on what nature makes for us. In the Celtic calendar, Lughnasadh marked the beginning of autumn, as the days will be shorter from then on. Lughnasadh is named after the Celtic god Lugh combined with the Old Gaelic word *násad*, which means "assemble." This sabbat is also called Lammas, which derives from the Old English word *half*, which means "loaf" or "loaf mass."

Lughnasadh Correspondences

COLORS The colors for this sabbat are yellow, gold, red, and burgundy. They recall golden wheat fields, berries, and the heat of the sun.

GRAIN During Lughnasadh, all grain is celebrated, from wheat to barley to oats. They will sustain humans and domestic animals during winter. Grain is seen as the generosity of Mother Nature, who gives us a part of her body to keep us alive.

SUNFLOWERS Their round, yellow flowers represent the golden solar disk. Their seeds are the embodiment of the fertility of the earth.

MAGICK It is the perfect moment for spells to manifest the results of our hard work during the rest of the year. Traditionally, couples, babies, and homes were blessed to ensure health and abundance.

FOOD Lughnasadh is deeply related to any food made from cereals, especially bread. You can also bake a cake or eat in-season fruits and vegetables.

Lughnasadh Activities

BAKE BREAD The first sheaf of the year is baked in a loaf and shared among the members of the community. This ritual promotes wealth and prosperity.

MAKE CORN DOLLIES These small figures are made with the last sheaf. They represent the spirit of the grain that will come back to the earth during spring. The dolly is buried in the fields once winter has passed to return the spirit of the grain to the earth. Corn dollies can be made from any cereal plant. The word *corn* initially meant "grain." When this tradition originated in Europe, people there had never seen corn, which is indigenous to the Americas.

ATTEND A MARKET OR FAIR As the harvest is starting and food is abundant, it is common to organize fairs to exchange and buy food and other items. To many pagans, it is important that the harvest is equally shared so nobody suffers from hunger during the winter.

FEAST Is there a better way to celebrate the abundance of the harvest than by eating? Traditional dishes feature in-season grains, fruits, and vegetables accompanied by different types of bread.

Lughnasadh Recipe: Seed Bread

Even though bread is baked for almost every sabbat, it takes on special relevance during Lughnasadh. Bread is a symbol of the harvest and also of sharing and taking care of the community. This recipe has different seeds in it to represent the seeds that will be collected during Lughnasadh and planted again after the winter.

Yield: 1 loaf

- 5 teaspoons (20 g) active dry yeast
- 2¾ cups (650 ml) lukewarm water, divided
- 7 cups (900 g) flour
- 1 tablespoon (15 g) salt
- 4 teaspoons (3 g) dried thyme
- 4 tablespoons (36 g) mixed seeds (sunflower, pumpkin, etc.)
- ¼ cup (60 ml) extra-virgin olive oil, plus more for the dough

In a small bowl, combine the yeast with 1 cup (235 ml) of the lukewarm water. Set it aside.

Mix the flour, salt, thyme, and seeds in a large bowl. Add the olive oil and the remaining 1¾ cups (410 ml) of water slowly. Add the yeast mixture and knead the dough for about 5 minutes. Put the dough in a bowl and oil its surface. Cover the bowl with a damp cloth and let the dough rise for 1 hour.

Take the dough out of the bowl and knead it again for 3 to 4 minutes. Let it rise a second time,until it doubles its size, about 1 hour.

Preheat the oven to 425°F (220°C, or gas mark 7). Line a baking sheet with parchment paper. Shape the loaf on the prepared baking sheet and bake for 25 to 30 minutes until it is golden brown. Check the loaf at the center with a toothpick. If it comes out clean, the bread is done. If not, return the loaf to the oven and watch it closely, checking it every couple of minutes until done.

Mabon

Mabon, like Ostara, celebrates the balance of life. However, this time we celebrate the triumph of darkness. During Mabon, the day is receding to make way for the night.

Mabon celebrates the second harvest. The leaves of the trees will start turning brown and golden soon, and all the grain has been harvested. It is the moment to pick the last fruits of summer and dry them to preserve them through winter. Flocks are led to their fold to protect them from the cold, and it is the start of the hunting season.

Mabon is a name that comes from Welsh mythology: *Mabon ap Modron* means "son of the mother." It was coined as the name of the autumn equinox by Aidan A. Kelly, founder of the Covenant of the Goddess, in the 1970s.

Mabon Correspondences

COLORS Mabon's palette announces that autumn is coming with browns, dark reds, and creams.

APPLES Apple seeds create a five-pointed star inside the fruit. To eat apples is to honor the five elements that bring balance to the universe. Planting an apple tree in your yard will protect your home from evil.

POMEGRANATES This autumn fruit is linked to Mabon because its shape and many seeds symbolize the fruits of Mother Earth. It is also linked to this season because of the myth of the goddess Persephone, who ate pomegranate seeds when she was in the underworld and had to spend half of the year there with Hades. When Persephone returns to the underworld each year, her mother, Demeter, the goddess of the fertility of the earth, becomes sad and nothing grows in nature, starting the autumn and winter seasons.

NUTS The season for collecting different nuts is starting. Walnuts, pine nuts, and acorns are some of the most popular ones. Nuts are a high-calorie food that was essential to survive the winter.

CORNUCOPIA The term comes from the Latin *cornu copiae*, which means "horn of plenty." It is a horn filled with many fruits, nuts, and flowers. It appears in Greek and Roman mythology associated with the goddess of the harvest as a symbol of abundance and good luck.

MAGICK Mabon is the time to let go of what no longer serves you. It is also a perfect moment to practice gratitude or cast protection and prosperity spells.

FOOD Grapes have been harvested and it is the perfect moment to make wine. Nuts, apples, squash, and autumn berries are present in many dishes, and cornbread and different types of pies are on the menu.

Mabon Activities

MAKE A MOBILE OF DRY LEAVES You can create a mobile using different colored leaves to welcome the autumn. Dip the leaves in beeswax or paraffin to make them last longer.

BE THANKFUL Make offerings to Mother Earth to show your gratitude for everything that she offers us. Fill a basket with fruit and other food to use as an offering. You can create a thanksgiving circle and make an offering to each of the five elements. (See "Casting a Circle"on page 159 to learn how to cast a circle and "Mother Earth, the Energy of the Universe, and the Five Elements" on page 18 to read about the five elements.)

MAKE A BESOM Besoms are brooms made from herbs or twigs tied to a wooden handle, creating a round shape. They can be used in cleansing and fertility rituals. Mabon is a perfect occasion to create your besom or mend the one you already have.

GO APPLE PICKING Apples are an essential part of this sabbat, and they are very versatile! Picking your own will give them more relevance in your craft. You can use them to make a pie, use them for decoration, use their seeds in protection spells, or give them as an offering. Apple tree branches can be used to make wands.

PRESERVE FOOD Now is the time to preserve food for the winter. There are many different techniques to do this, from canning vegetables to drying fruits, making jam, and making pickled vegetables.

SHARE FOOD As the cold part of the year is approaching, it is traditional to donate food to those in need, especially canned or dried food, which can last all winter.

Mabon Recipe: Apple Mille-Feuille

This delicious dessert is a reinterpretation of mille-feuille, *which translates to "thousand sheets." Here, we exchange puff pastry for baked apples.*

Yield: 4 servings

4 apples
½ lemon
¾ cup (100 g) shelled walnuts
1 tablespoon (13 g) sugar
1 teaspoon ground cinnamon
Honey, to taste

Preheat the oven to 350⁰F (180⁰C, or gas mark 4). Line a baking sheet with parchment paper.

Peel and core the apples, then cut them into thin slices. Squeeze the lemon over them.

Chop the walnuts. Mix them in a bowl with the sugar and cinnamon. Place a cooking ring on the prepared baking sheet and start stacking layers of apple and walnut mixture until you have filled the cooking ring. Remove the ring and do the same with the rest of the apple slices. Pour a bit of honey over the apples and bake for 30 minutes until the apples are soft.

Samhain

Samhain is the witches' New Year. It is the end of a cycle and the beginning of a new one. However, it is not only linked to the seasons' cycle but also to the life cycle. It celebrates life and death.

Samhain is a date when the spirit realm and the world of the living are almost completely connected as the veil between them thins. This bridge between worlds allows the spirits of the loved ones who have passed away to come to visit their families and friends. Pagans set up altars and offerings to make them feel welcome and remembered.

It is also the third and last harvest. The Earth gives us her last fruits, and this is the last opportunity to preserve food to survive the winter. Some animals are slaughtered during this time of the year to preserve their meat for the cold months. The dark half of the year is starting.

The name Samhain originates from the Gaelic word for "summer's end." With the growth of Christianity in Europe, Samhain was incorporated into Christian celebrations as All Hallows' Eve, which later became Halloween.

Samhain Correspondences

COLORS During this sabbat, altars and homes are decorated with black, orange, and white items.

PUMPKINS These fruits are a big part of the celebration of Samhain. As they are in season, many recipes contain them. They are also used to create traditional jack-o'-lanterns.

BESOM The besoms made during Mabon are used to sweep away the dry leaves as well as the old energy from all the past sabbats. This makes room for the new energy that the upcoming turn of the wheel brings.

SPOOKY DECORATIONS Skeletons, ghosts, scythes, and other decorations related to death and the spirit realm are a reminder of the cycle of life and death's inevitability.

MAGICK This sabbat is focused on honoring the dead, especially our ancestors. It is common to celebrate rituals to remember them or to contact them. It is also a good moment to meditate about the cycle of life, death, and rebirth and to practice divination.

FOOD The recipes related to Samhain usually contain pumpkins or squashes as well as nuts, wine, and cider. Some examples are soul cakes, pumpkin cakes, and mulled wine.

Samhain Activities

HONOR YOUR ANCESTORS Create an altar with photos of family members and friends who have passed away. Include some of their objects or things that they would have liked, as well as flowers and candles. Dedicate a moment to remembering them. This should not be a sad ritual. It is an intimate moment to share memories and feel the presence of their spirits.

HONOR THE FORGOTTEN DEAD Some spirits are not so lucky to have someone who remembers them. Reserve a small part of your altar to make them an offering.

MAKE JACK-O'-LANTERNS Carving faces in pumpkins or turnips and placing a candle inside to create a lantern is a longstanding tradition. It wasn't until the nineteenth century that they began to be used as Halloween and Samhain decorations.

HAVE A DUMB SUPPER This ceremony consists of a special dinner where all the family is invited, including those who have passed away. Plates and cutlery are set for everybody and the dinner is eaten in silence.

PRACTICE DIVINATION As the veil between worlds is thinner, Samhain is a perfect opportunity to practice divination.

Samhain Recipe: Pumpkin Jam

As you may have guessed, Samhain's recipe is about pumpkins. However, I wanted to do something a bit different, so I present you with this pumpkin jam, which is a perfect accompaniment to strong cheeses.

Yield: 3 cups (975 g) jam

1½ pounds (750 g) pumpkin, peeled and seeded
Zest and juice from 1 orange
1¼ cups (250 g) sugar
1 cinnamon stick
Water, if needed

Cut the pumpkin into a small dice and place it in a large bowl. In a medium bowl, combine the orange zest and juice, sugar, and cinnamon and pour the mixture over the pumpkin. Mix well and let it sit overnight.

Remove the cinnamon stick, transfer the mixture to a nonstick pot, and let it simmer for about 1 hour or until it has the desired jam-like consistency. Be sure to check the jam as it simmers and add water if needed. Let the jam cool completely before eating.

Things I Wish Someone Had Told Me

The Wheel of the Year and the Equator

Living near the equator and following the wheel can be difficult, as the seasons are not as differentiated from one another as they are in other parts of the globe. Places in the northern hemisphere near the equator may fit the southern Wheel of the Year better and vice versa.

My advice is to follow the Wheel of the Year version that fits best with where you live. In the end, the main purpose of the wheel is to celebrate and adapt to the natural cycle of the seasons, not to adapt the seasons to our celebrations.

Celebrating the Sabbats on the Go

Sometimes you are traveling, working, or simply really busy and can't organize something special to celebrate a sabbat. I have been there many times. First of all, it is important to understand that if you can't celebrate it, you can't, and there is nothing wrong with that. The sabbats are supposed to be a celebration, a way to get in touch with Mother Earth, not an obligation.

Keep in mind that there are activities that are simple and don't take much time that you can do to celebrate. Go outside and reflect on the cycle of the seasons and the moment in the year. Have you observed the subtle changes in nature? Take a minute to stop and meditate. Find a moment of calm in your busy routine and feel the spin of the wheel. This is a perfectly valid—and quick—way to celebrate a sabbat.

CHAPTER 5

Crystals

The power of crystals is well known among witches. Their unique vibrations and capacity to modify the energy that goes through them make them perfect for magickal workings. They are used to cast spells and perform rituals, but they are also included in everyday life.

For beginners, it can be a bit confusing to understand how to use the energy of crystals. Crystals, along with herbs, come directly from Mother Earth and, because of it, they contain her energy. They are powerful tools that allow us to channel and modify energy, from us and from others.

Each crystal has valuable properties and uses that depend on their composition, shape, color, etc... It is worth your time to learn more about them and the ways to make good use of their benefits.
In this chapter, I included 10 of the most popular crystals, the reason behind the different shapes of crystals. You will read about the different techniques to use crystals, from cleansing them to programing them and creating crystal grids.

Essential Crystals

As with other tools needed for witchcraft, crystals are neither completely essential nor indispensable. You only need a handful of crystals with different correspondences and properties to begin exploring their power. Here is a list of some of the most popular crystals to help you create a versatile crystal kit.

Amethyst

Amethyst is a variety of quartz. Its purple color is caused by iron deposits, irradiation, and other impurities. These impurities give amethysts their range of colors.

Amethysts are great healers. They are recommended to soothe stress, promote mental peace, and filter negative thoughts. It is said that amethyst can purify your inner energy and the energy that comes to you. Meditating with a piece of amethyst is one of the best ways to promote a healthy rest. It is also advised to wear some type of jewelry that allows the amethyst to be in contact with your skin.

If you are trying to improve your psychic abilities, amethyst will be your best friend. Its color and vibrations are a helping hand when tuning in to your intuition and stimulating your creativity. Place one on your altar to prepare it for a divination session or put one under your pillow to promote prophetic dreams.

The ancient Greeks and Romans believed that amethyst could prevent drunkenness, and in the medieval ages, Christian bishops wore amethyst rings to represent and affirm their chastity vow. Because of these traditions, amethyst has also been used for recovery from addiction.

To keep your amethyst in perfect condition, do not use harsh chemical cleaners. Clean it only with warm, soapy water. Let it air-dry or use a soft towel. Store the crystal away from direct sunlight and heat to avoid fading and damage. Keep it wrapped in a soft cloth to prevent scratches.

Black Tourmaline

Also called schorl, black tourmaline is the most abundant variety of tourmaline, making up almost 95 percent of the total. It owes its characteristic black color to its sodium and iron content.

Black tourmaline is one of the most powerful crystals for protection. It is used in purifying

rituals to eliminate negative energies and to fight against psychic attacks and energy vampires. An easy, yet powerful, purifying ritual is a ritual bath that incorporates black tourmaline and black salt.

This is a strong grounding crystal and can be a part of any grounding ritual, particularly if you are going on a walk-in nature. If you are feeling tired, meditate with black tourmaline to regain your balance. It is also said that black tourmaline can absorb electromagnetic smog, so keep one near your computer or other electronics that you use often.

To take care of your black tourmaline, avoid harsh chemical cleaners. Clean it with warm, soapy water and avoid exposing it to high temperatures.

Citrine

Think of citrine as the "next step" of amethyst. Any amethyst crystal exposed to extreme conditions of heat and pressure for a long time will become citrine. The iron deposits in citrine crystals are oxidized, making its color change from purple to yellow. Nowadays, most of the citrine that is sold is artificially created from amethyst or smoky quartz.

Citrine embodies the energy of the sun. It is used to balance energies because it transforms negative energies into positive ones. It radiates positive energy and happiness, and it helps with self-esteem. Citrine also boosts your creativity and intuition.

It is called the "merchant stone" because it is said to have the ability to bring money to your life and make your business successful while protecting you from jealousy. One of the simplest spells to invite money into your life is placing a citrine with some coins in your home (or business, if you own one) and lighting a green candle.

Do not use harsh chemical cleaners on your citrine. Wash it with warm, soapy water and let it air-dry. Store it somewhere protected from any scratches or knocks. Do not expose it to direct sunlight or heat; its color will fade, and the crystal will be permanently damaged.

Clear Quartz

Quartz is the second most common mineral on Earth. There are many varieties, and the impurities they contain give them different colors. Clear quartz is a quartz without impurities.

Clear quartz is one of the most versatile crystals. It is often called the all-purpose crystal because it is easily programmed and can substitute for any other crystal. It is commonly used to amplify the properties of other crystals or to activate crystal grids.

It is said to purify your energy, bringing mental clarity and creativity. Clear quartz helps improve your divination abilities and your focus. This crystal is also used as an offering to the dead, so it can be placed on an altar or a grave.

Do not use harsh chemical cleaners on your quartz. You just need to wash it with warm, soapy water and let it air-dry. Store it in a soft cloth to avoid scratches and avoid prolonged exposure to sunlight or heat.

Fluorite

Fluorite is made from calcium fluoride, and it comes in a wide range of colors. The phenomenon of fluorescence is named after this crystal, as many of its varieties present this property under ultraviolet light.

Fluorite soothes chaotic minds. It helps you to be more flexible when making a decision and to stay calm when facing an obstacle. It is also commonly used to boost creativity and improve focus.

It can be used as a protective crystal against negative energies and electromagnetic smog. You can use it to cleanse auras, but it can quickly absorb many unwanted energies. Cleanse it often.

Fluorite is classified as a soft crystal, making it especially important to protect it from scratches. Prolonged exposure to sunlight can fade its color. Do not use harsh chemical cleaners. You can wash your fluorite with warm, soapy water and a dedicated soft cloth. (Do not use the cloth for anything else.)

This crystal is toxic. Wash your hands after handling it. Do not drink water that has been in direct contact with fluorite. Always wear a mask and protect your eyes if you engrave fluorite.

Hematite

Hematite is a mineral from iron oxide. Its name comes from the ancient Greek *haimatitēs lithos*, literally "blood-red stone." It has a black, shiny color, and when pulverized it becomes red and can be used as a pigment. Do not confuse hematite with bloodstone; they have different compositions and properties.

Due to the red color of its powder, it was believed that hematite was made from the blood of ancient warriors. This generated the belief that hematite promotes courage and absorbs negative feelings and toxic emotions. Today, it is commonly used for emotional healing.

It is said that just by touching hematite, you will feel more centered, balanced, and grounded. Meditate daily with it and carry one with you for those moments when you need stability and clear thinking. It is especially useful when grounding outdoors, as it helps you reconnect with Mother Earth.

To take care of hematite, do not use harsh chemical cleaners. Clean it with warm, soapy water. Make sure to rinse it well. This crystal is rather soft and brittle, so store it in a soft cloth away from harder crystals.

Rose Quartz

Rose quartz is a very common variety of quartz that shows a pink hue. This is usually caused by the presence of titanium, iron, or manganese, but other elements can also be present.

Rose quartz is the crystal of all types of love: friendship, familial love, self-love, and—of course—romantic love. It is said to help develop stronger bonds, as well as resolve anger and disappointment.

This crystal is very appreciated for its use in self-love rituals. It improves self-esteem and self-confidence, releases stress, and promotes calm. It is commonly used in elixirs, glamours (page 163), and other beauty spells. If you are planning on buying a facial roller, try one made from rose quartz.

Do not use harsh chemical cleaners on rose quartz. Wash it with warm, soapy water and let it air-dry. It can be damaged by direct sunlight or heat. Store it with care in a soft cloth to avoid scratches.

Selenite

Selenite is a type of transparent gypsum. The word *selenite* comes from the Greek word *selēnitēs*, from *lithos* (stone) and *selēnē* (moon), meaning "stone of the moon."

As its name suggests, selenite has a strong connection with the moon and its cycles. It is used to create safe spaces and crystal grids. To keep unwanted energies away from your magickal workings, create a selenite grid around your altar.

Selenite is known for its cleansing properties and ability to channel energy. It is used to create wands and other kinds of magickal items. It also works well for cleansing other objects. Place a piece of selenite overnight with your crystals or divination tools to cleanse them.

Selenite is a very soft mineral. Do not use harsh chemical cleaners. Do not submerge it. It can be dissolved by water. If it gets wet, allow it to air-dry. Selenite can be scratched easily. Be sure to store it separately from other crystals.

Smoky Quartz

This variety of quartz has a wide color range, from yellowish semitransparent crystals to almost-black opaque crystals. The most common color is brown.

You will find some of these crystals where clear quartz and smoky quartz are mixed, creating a beautiful design that looks like a wisp of smoke frozen in time inside the crystal. This type of smoky quartz is the best for cleansing, detoxifying, and protecting. Smoky quartz absorbs negative energies and can also cleanse and transform them. Because of this, it is important to cleanse your smoky quartz regularly.

This crystal is especially valuable for meditation and grounding yourself, particularly when doing spirit work. To consciously release negative energies to Mother Earth, hold faceted or natural points of smoky quartz in each hand pointed down toward the ground.

Do not use harsh chemical cleaners on your smoky quartz. To clean it, wash with warm, soapy water. Wrap it in a soft cloth to avoid scratches and do not expose it to heat and sunlight for long periods of time.

Tiger's Eye

Tiger's eye is, once again, a variety of quartz. The formation process of tiger's eye generates an optical effect called chatoyancy that makes it resemble a tiger's eye.

This crystal is said to bring the qualities of the tiger to your life. It promotes focus, patience, and courage. It can help you make better decisions through quick thinking and emotional stability. It can also soothe tension after an argument.

Tiger's eye is commonly used to attract money and improve business relationships and decisions. It is also a help during public performances and competitions. It is the crystal of success, helping you stabilize your mind and keep a positive attitude.

Do not use harsh chemical cleaners on your tiger's eye. Wash with warm, soapy water. Avoid spraying it with perfume or hair spray, which can damage the crystal and make it lose its shine.

Crystal Shapes

Crystals come in many different shapes—some are naturally created and others are man-made. The properties and correspondences of the crystals don't change based on their shape, but some shapes are more suitable for certain energy work than others.

Experiment with different crystal shapes and see what works best for you. These are some of the most common ones.

Cluster

This shape is created naturally when many crystals grow together from the same matrix. Clusters have many energy-emitting points, and that may seem chaotic. However, cluster crystals work as a whole, allowing energy to be emitted in several directions. It is believed that this amplifies the energy of the crystal.

Crystal clusters are usually placed at home or at work to amplify the energy that you want to create for that space. For example, if you want to attract money into your business, use a citrine cluster. If you want to create a loving atmosphere in your bedroom, use a rose quartz cluster. They can also be used as center pieces for crystal grids.

Crystal Point

This popular shape works as an energy amplifier to magnify energy and intentions. Because of this, crystal points are placed in the center of crystal grids and altars or in the corners. They are very versatile crystals and are often used to manifest intentions because they allow you to direct energy.

To recharge yourself, hold a crystal pointing outward in your projecting hand and one pointing inward in your receptive hand (see page 30). This will stimulate the energy flow. Clear quartz is one of the most suitable crystals for this.

Points can be natural or man-made, and some witches prefer one type over the other because they have different energies.

Double Terminated Crystal

These crystals are double ended, which means that they have two "points." Double terminated crystals are known for having a bidirectional energy flow, one for each termination.

They are great connecting crystals in crystal grids, as they double the direction the energy flows, allowing the rest of the crystals to be connected. This type of energy also makes them perfect for finding balance.

Double terminated crystals can be natural or artificial. Many witches and healers who work with crystals prefer the natural ones, as their double energy flow is more present.

Raw Crystals

Also called rough crystals, raw crystals are in their native state. They haven't been polished or shaped. They come in different shapes and sizes, including cluster crystals and some pointed and double terminated crystals.

They are among the most powerful crystals, as their energy is intact. They add a special connection with Mother Earth in all rituals that include them. They usually take the middle place in crystal grids, acting as a link between other crystals.

Do not create elixirs with raw crystals. Even if the main crystal is not toxic, it may contain toxic impurities.

Sphere

Perfectly round, polished crystals are also known as crystal balls. Their best-known use is in divination. They are used for scrying, a type of divination where you gaze into a polished surface (see "Scrying" on page 120). However, their relationship with divination goes further, as they can be included in your practice or rituals to open your inner eye and boost your intuition.

The smooth and round surface allows gentle energy to be projected symmetrically in all directions, allowing it to reach throughout the room. This makes them perfect to balance energies and promote harmony. For grounding and balance, meditate while holding a sphere in each hand.

Keep in mind that crystal spheres will need a stand. You don't want them rolling around!

Tumbled Stones

These small, polished stones are one of the most common shapes for crystals. They are usually smaller and it takes less work to create them, so they are more affordable and accessible for beginners. If you feel drawn to a specific crystal but you are not sure whether it would work for you, then a tumbled stone is one of your best options.

Tumbled stones radiate energy from their entire surface. Their size makes them perfect to carry with you, to create crystal grids, or to include in sachets or bottle spells.

Others

You can find many other crystal shapes, such as pyramids, wands, skulls, animals, and hearts, and each one has different applications. Try out different shapes to find the ones that best suit you.

How to Use Crystals

Crystals need to be prepared before using them. This will boost their effectiveness and help prevent any unwanted energy from interfering with your intentions.

Cleansing Crystals

Crystals are tools that always have a flow of energy through them. This also means that they can clog with built-up energy. They can also be contaminated by negative energy.

Cleaning and cleansing are different things in witchcraft; cleaning removes "dirt," while cleansing works with energies. I describe some of the most common techniques to cleanse magick tools in chapter 9.

For crystals, you should cleanse them right after you buy or receive them and cleanse them regularly to keep them effective. If you use them daily, do this every week. If you use them once in a while, do it after each use.

Be sure to choose a technique that doesn't damage your crystals. Water can affect the composition of some crystals. (See the cleaning techniques for each type of crystal earlier in this chapter.)

Charging Crystals

Crystals may also feel drained or dull after being used. When this happens, it is time to charge them. Usually, charging a crystal is the step that follows cleansing it because it restores the energy of the crystal. Be sure to research your crystals before charging them. Some techniques, such as sunlight, may damage them. Chapter 9 provides details about how to charge your magick tools.

Programming Crystals

Crystals are believed to have a special capacity to retain energies. We work with crystals by programming them—we imbue them with our intentions. It is not essential to program crystals to use them, but it is useful when you want them to help you achieve a specific goal.

Some witches don't incorporate this practice in their craft. They believe that there is no need to program crystals, as they react to our needs. Personally, I believe that programming crystals helps focus their energy and increases the chances of success, making them more effective.

To program a crystal, you need to communicate with it to open your mind and heart. Hold the crystal in your hands or in your projecting hand. Quiet your mind and focus on your intention. Send that image or thought to your crystal. Do this through visualization, seeing your intention as a warm light that flows from you through your arms and hands, arriving to your crystal, filling it and making it glow. With time and practice you will be able to feel the energy flow.

As you travel your path, experiment and explore to find the technique that works best for you. Also be sure to follow the natural correspondences of the crystal. Not all crystals can be programmed to achieve all types of goals. In fact, most are suitable to work only toward one type (e.g., success, health, relationships, business, etc.). Clear quartz is an exception to this rule, as it can be programmed with all types of intentions.

If you want to cancel the programming, cleanse the crystal, and it will be ready to program again. Don't be afraid of programming a crystal several times. It is important that your crystals aren't clogged with negative energy when you use them.

Crystal Grids

Crystal grids arrange crystals into geometric patterns. They use shapes and geometry to interconnect crystals and create a strong link between them and your intention. It is believed that crystal grids make your rituals more powerful than using crystals separately.

First, choose the crystals that you are going to use to manifest your intention. The minimum number is usually four, but you can use more if you want to. Try to choose a number of crystals that allows you to create a symmetrical shape. The most common crystal shapes used are tumbled crystals, and crystal points are added in the places of higher energy at the center or the corners.

Then, choose a pattern that resonates with you and your goals. There are many to choose from, including heart shapes, geometric shapes, spirals, and mandalas. Create them yourself by drawing on a piece of paper or search for one online. There are shops specializing in crystals and witchcraft that sell altar plates with crystal grids on them.

To begin your ritual, cleanse the crystals, grid, and space. Choose a main crystal that matches your intention. Place the main crystal in the center. Continue working your way out, placing the smaller crystals. Some people like to write their intention on a small piece of paper, fold it, and place it under the center crystal.

Activate your crystal grid with a quartz crystal point, your finger, or a wand. Touch all the stones and connect them with the surrounding ones, much like "connecting the dots." You are creating energetic lines. Do this in precise order and don't break the line.

Your crystal grid is finished! Take a moment to reflect on your intention, feel its energy, and give thanks. Leave the crystals in place until your intention is fulfilled. Retrace the lines if you feel that the energy is weakening.

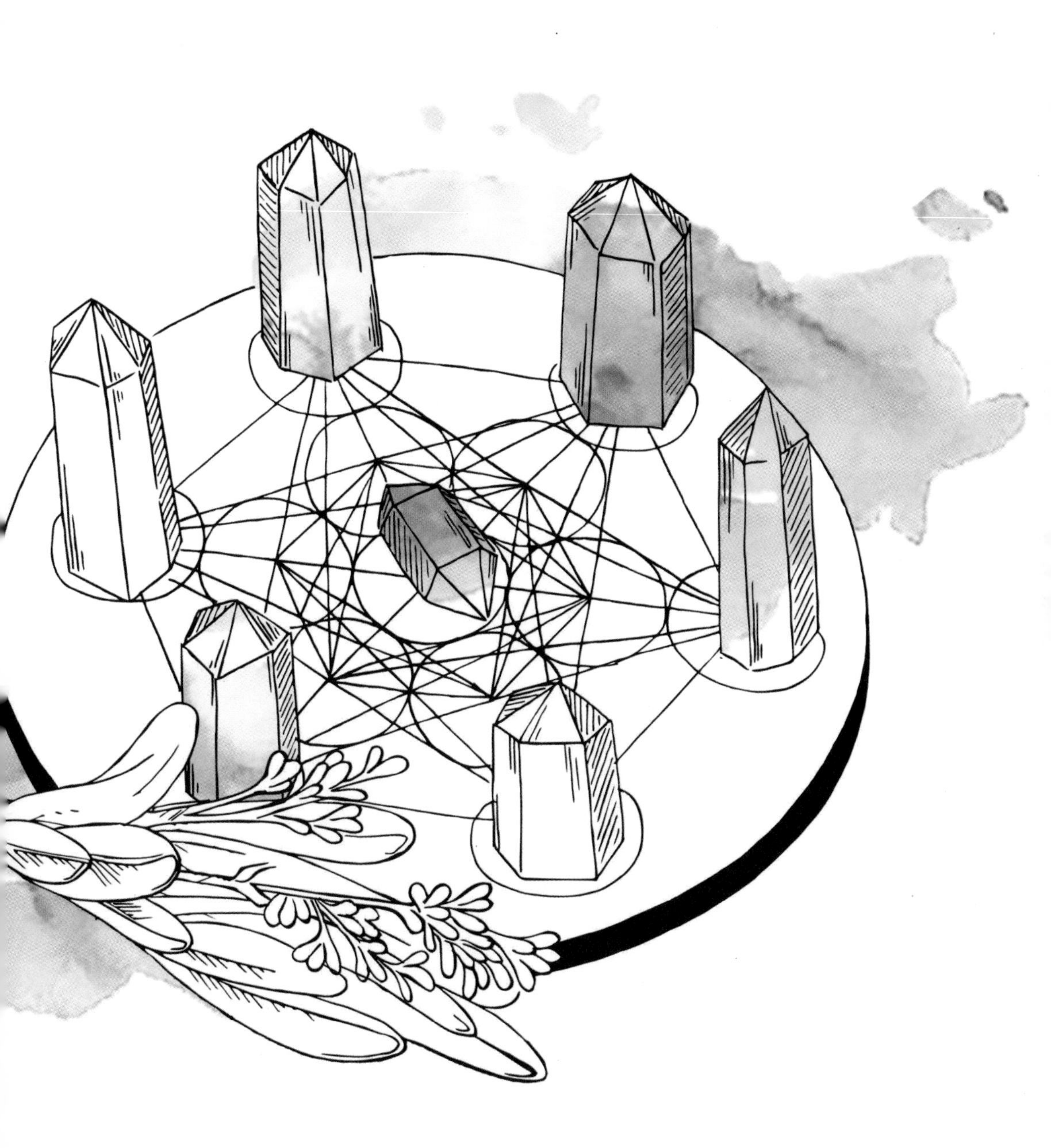

Toxicity

Always make sure that you are handling your tools and materials safely. Crystals have different chemical compositions, and some of them contain toxic compounds in their crystal structures. Some may not be safe to touch, use for elixirs, or have in contact with your mucous membranes or eyes.

It is not necessary to expose your elixirs or potions to direct contact with crystals in order to charge them. Remember: Crystals project their energy. Place them close to the container with your elixir, and it will have the same effect.

When you are carving any crystals, avoid touching your eyes or mouth when handling them. Always wear respiratory protection to avoid inhaling dust.

Be sure to do your research before using any new crystal to avoid unwanted effects.

Things I Wish Someone Had Told Me

Combine Crystals with Other Items

Crystals can be very powerful used on their own or with other crystals to boost or modify their energy. I personally prefer to combine crystals with herbs and other magickal items. For me, the energy from a spell that draws on energies from different sources is more complete.

Try brewing herbal teas with a water that has been charged with a crystal to create a powerful potion or elixir. Or craft a wand from a branch and add a pointed crystal at the end; the wood will channel your energy, and the crystal will focus it.

CHAPTER 6

Herbs

Herbal medicine has always been closely linked to witchcraft, and sometimes the line that divides both fields can be blurry. Although the type of witchcraft that focuses on Mother Earth and especially plants is called Green Witchcraft, many other branches incorporate them in their craft. I love using herbs in my spells because they allow me to combine witchcraft with traditional medicine.

Mother Earth offers us resources to heal our mind and spirit. By creating a connection with her and attuning with Nature, we renewal our balance. Herbs are a gift that, when incorporated into our craft, helps us to materialize our intention and achieve our goals. However, as many other relationships in witchcraft, this is an exchange. When using what Mother Earth offers, we should be grateful and take care of her being as environmentally friendly as we can.

In this chapter you will find the magickal properties of 10 popular herbs as well as their uses in traditional medicine and some notions on how to grow them. You will also learn about different ways to incorporate herbs to your craft, with examples of each one of them.

Essential Herbs

Every witch who works with herbs has a list of the ones that are indispensable—and so do I. Because my witchcraft is rooted in the Celtiberian pagan traditions of the Iberian Peninsula, all the herbs listed are plants that can be found easily there. Most of these plants are adapted to the Mediterranean weather and soil; however, they can be grown under other conditions with just a few adjustments. Plus, most of them are widely available as cooking herbs and spices.

Basil (*Ocimum basilicum*)

In witchcraft, basil is a strong herb for protecting the home, bringing happiness, and promoting reconciliations. It is also used to enhance psychic abilities through mental clarity, especially lucid dreaming and astral traveling.

Basil is appreciated for its flavor, and it has been carefully cultivated to create different varieties, such as lemon basil and sweet basil. Basil also has healing uses. It helps with nausea and upset stomach because of its anti-inflammatory properties. It is also rich in antioxidants and vitamin K. Basil is used to reduces stress and boost the immune system as well.

Basil is native to Central Africa and Southeast Asia, but nowadays it is grown almost all around the globe, from Canada to New Zealand. It prefers hot and dry conditions, but it can be kept in a greenhouse. Basil will behave as an annual plant and die with the first frost. It needs good drainage and 6 to 8 hours of sunlight. With the appropriate conditions, it can reach from 1 to 6 feet (30 cm to 2 m) tall.

Bay Laurel (*Laurus nobilis*)

It is said that if you write a wish on a bay leaf and then burn it, your wish will come true. This herb is used in spells that involve success and protection, and it is also used to enhance psychic abilities. Bay laurel had a prominent place in classical Greco-Roman culture, as the well-known laurel wreaths were a symbol of status and victory. The oracle at Delphi chewed bay laurel leaves to achieve a prophetic state.

Also called sweet laurel or bay tree, bay laurel has fragrant leaves that are widely appreciated as a food seasoning. The essential oil is used effectively in creams to treat dandruff and joint pain. This is because it contains an antiseptic substance as well as a mild narcotic.

Bay laurel is native to the more humid regions of the Mediterranean Basin. You can find it as a tree or large shrub. Bay laurel is a drought-tolerant plant that prefers well-drained soil.

Calendula (*Calendula officinalis*)

Because of the shape of its flowers, calendula has a strong relationship with the sun. It is used to protect houses from evil, and if burned it is used to consecrate items. It is a good addition to sleep sachets and love spells because it promotes psychic abilities, love, and constancy.

Calendula's beautiful flowers and long flowering period have made it a popular plant for gardens. These flowers also have been the best friend of those with skin problems since ancient times. Calendula is widely used in cosmetics and skin-soothing creams. Its antibacterial, antiseptic, antifungal, and anti-inflammatory properties make it a perfect remedy for several skin problems.

It needs a poor to average, well-drained soil. It prefers full sun, but not too much heat. The best moment to harvest its flowers is just after they have opened in the morning. The flowers usually are covered in a sticky substance, so it is best to wear gloves.

Chamomile (*Chamaemelum nobile*)

In witchcraft, chamomile is a very positive herb. Like calendula, it is related to the sun because of its shape. Chamomile is used in rituals to promote calm, peace, and love. It is an herb for reconciliation, with others or with yourself.

This daisy-like plant is appreciated for its fragrance and for its extensive magickal and

medicinal properties. Chamomile is anti-inflammatory. In traditional medicine, it is used to treat nausea, upset stomach, and irritated skin. Chamomile rinse has been used since ancient times as a natural way to lighten hair color. Note: It has been cataloged as unsafe for pregnant and breastfeeding mothers.

Chamomile likes dry, well-drained soil and needs little fertilizer or watering. It prefers part shade, but it can adapt to full sun. Plant it near other plants as a natural way to reduce pests in your garden.

Lavender (*Lavandula angustifolia*)

The magickal properties of lavender include helping with insomnia and nightmares, as well as providing mental clarity and calm. It is used in rituals to promote fertility and to aid in divination. It is a common offering during Litha and when a child is born.

Lavender is well known for its fragrant scent and purple flowers. There are many varieties of lavender; some are different species, but from the same genus. Lavender has been used to help with insomnia and stress because of its soothing smell. Lavender infusions are used to calm digestive issues and headaches, and if applied to the scalp can help with some types of hair loss.

Lavender should be planted about 2 feet (61 cm) apart in moderately fertile soil with good drainage. It is better to harvest it when half of the buds have opened. If you have the space, create a beautiful lavender path that will attract bees, butterflies, and other pollinators.

Mint (*Mentha spicata*)

In witchcraft, mint is deeply related to communication and used as an herb to promote courage, eloquence, and persuasion. This herb can also enhance your ability to communicate with the spirit realm. Greek mythology links it to the underworld, and it is used in rituals related to death.

One of the best experiences in a garden is touching some fresh mint and being rewarded with that distinctive smell. There are many different varieties of mint, and they generally have the same uses. My personal favorite is chocolate mint. Mint contains an organic compound called menthol, which acts as a local anesthetic, antispasmodic, antipruritic, and decongestant. Because of this, mint is a great help in treating nasal congestion, sore throat, muscular pain, itchiness, and digestive discomfort.

Mint is easier to grow from a cutting than from seed. If you place a cutting in a container with water, it will develop roots. With the right conditions, mint can spread like wildfire, so my advice is to contain it in a pot.

Mugwort (*Artemisia vulgaris*)

This plant is strongly related to femininity, labor, and menstrual cycles. It has been traditionally used to promote prophetic dreams and astral projections. Its strong relationship with divination makes it perfect to cleanse and bless tools used for that purpose.

Mugwort contains thujone, a toxic oil that can cause severe health problems, and it can even be lethal. However, in small doses, mugwort has been traditionally used to help with irregular periods and other menstrual problems, as it can start periods. It is also commonly used to treat different digestive problems and to stimulate the appetite. Mugwort is said to be a mild hallucinogen and sedative for some people. It is classified as unsafe for pregnant women. Mugwort should not be continuously used for more than a week.

Mugwort is a perennial herb that prefers a sunny spot with well-drained soil. It is best to use gloves when handling it to avoid absorbing the toxic oil through the skin. Be careful: Mugwort is an invasive and harmful plant in some places.

Rosemary (*Rosmarinus officinalis*)

Rosemary is used in rituals to cleanse, bless, and purify places, objects, or people. The most common ways to do so are by burning it or using it in ritual baths. It is especially useful to cleanse spaces where a long illness or a misfortune has taken place.

With a strong smell and flavor, rosemary is the perfect addition to any garden or kitchen. Its bluish flowers attract pollinators and give it a distinctive touch of color. In traditional medicine, rosemary is used to treat digestive problems, particularly those related to muscle spasms. Topically, it is used to relieve muscle pain and circulatory problems and as a healing agent.

Rosemary grows well in sandy, well-drained soil. Plants prefer full sun with a good air circulation and can tolerate high temperatures. It is best to take them inside if the winter is going to be very cold.

Note: It is not recommended to apply rosemary to open wounds. It is not advised to ingest it for longer periods than two weeks and not to use it topically for longer than four weeks. Ingesting big dosses of rosemary can be toxic.

Stinging Nettle (*Urtica dioica*)

This plant is used in witchcraft to disrupt negative energies. It cleanses energies in general, so it is suitable to cleanse objects, people, and places. Nettle is especially useful for weakening and breaking curses. Its smoke is used to keep unwanted entities away and to bless an athame (page 29). You can incorporate stinging nettle into blessed water or anointing oil to bless athames or simply burn stinging nettles and pass the athame over the smoke.

Stinging nettle has a bad reputation because when touched the hairs inject histamine and other substances that cause pain. If collected with caution, this versatile plant can be used for food, medicine, magick, and even textiles. Stinging nettle rash was used as a relief for joint pain. Once the first pain and itch of the stinging subsides, it relieves the inflammation of the joints, and with it, the pain. Nowadays, there are creams that contain stinging nettle and have a similar effect without the rash. Nettle also has diuretic properties and is a natural source of sodium and vitamin C.

Nettle prefers a moist and rich soil, with 1 foot (30 cm) between each plant. Harvest stinging nettle carefully, as the stingers can pierce thin fabric. To eliminate the hairs, blanch or crush the leaves before using them. Stinging nettle can cause allergic reactions and should be avoided by pregnant and breastfeeding women.

Thyme (*Thymus vulgaris*)

Since ancient times, thyme has been associated with healing, protection, and courage. It was used as an antidote for poisons, to give courage to soldiers going into battle, and even as a remedy for the Black Death. Thyme still has the same applications in witchcraft nowadays. Its smoke promotes courage and attracts good health. It is placed in coffins to ensure a safe passage to the otherworld. Fairies love its smell, so it is said that blowing thyme leaves can help attract them and that if you find a patch of wild thyme, it's a sign that faeries danced during the night in that spot.

Thyme contains a chemical compound known as thymol that is a powerful antiseptic and anti-inflammatory. This makes it perfect to treat small wounds or skin problems, such as acne, as well as a sore throat.

As a Mediterranean plant, thyme prefers sun and good drainage. It doesn't need fertilizer, but it should be protected from freezing. The best time to harvest it is right before flowering. You should give the plant a couple of years to establish after planting before you harvest from it.

How to Use Herbs

Herbs are incredibly versatile, and there are many ways to incorporate them into your craft. They can be used in herbal baths, potions, and smoke. And herbs have their own magickal correspondences based on their energy and the type of intention that they boost.

Herbal Baths

Healing illness by bathing in water is a practice that has been used since the ancient Greeks and Romans. Witchcraft expanded it to include energy work and magick. Herbal baths can include hot and cold water, showers, steams, or even mud, but they are not limited to that. Using mineral baths and adding herbs, crystals, and oils to water all offer opportunities to bring traditional medicine and witchcraft together. Be as creative as you wish mixing the power of herbs with the power of water.

Herb Combinations for Baths

- A bath with chamomile will help remove any negative energy attached to you and release your pain and anger.
- Rosemary is a great addition to your bath when you are looking for a deep energy cleansing and blessing.
- Rose petals will help you with any matter related to beauty or self-esteem.
- A bath bomb with some drops of mint essential oil is perfect to recharge and eliminate energy blockages.

Most spells that include herbal baths combine them with visualization to boost their effectiveness. Visualize the energy that you want to receive coming from the water and entering your body. Feel the water washing away the energy that you no longer need.

When you try herbal baths at home, place the herbs and other ingredients in a small sachet to avoid all the mess in your bathtub. The sachet should be made of a permeable natural fiber that allows the interchange of oils, energy, and other properties of the herbs with the bathwater. A large metal tea strainer works wonders for this purpose, too. If you prefer to see yourself surrounded by herbs, try a drain strainer to keep them from clogging the pipes.

Burning Herbs

Herbs are usually burned for cleansing purposes and for blessing rituals. To burn herbs, you can make herb bundles or use charcoal.

To create an herb bundle, gather fresh herbs that are about 6 inches (15 cm) long. Place them together facing the same direction to create a bundle about 1½ inches (4 cm) thick. Tie the herbs together with some twine or cotton yarn in a crisscross pattern. Do not use plastic: it won't burn well and the smoke will interfere with the purpose of the bundle. Hang the bundle by the end of the stems and let them air-dry.

If you prefer to use a mix of loose dry leaves, you just need a charcoal disk and a fireproof container. Light the disk, place it in a container, and sprinkle the herb blend over it. Always make sure that the container is fireproof and never leave your burning herbs unattended.

I prefer loose herb blends to herb bundles. It feels more natural for my craft. I like to prepare mixes beforehand and store them in jars, so they are ready to use when I need them.

My Favorite Herb Blend for Regular Cleansing

- 1 part cedar
- 2 parts rosemary
- 2 parts lavender
- ½ part frankincense

Make sure that the herbs you want to burn haven't been treated with pesticides or other harmful chemicals, as they would release small amounts of toxic fumes when burned.

Herbal Sachets and Jars

Sachets and jar spells both start from the same premise: They concentrate the magickal energy in a container to make it more powerful. Sachets are permeable and allow an interchange of energy with the exterior. Spell jars are closed and concentrate all the magick energy inside. If you are using sachets, they sometimes need to be "fed," recharging them with your intent and some fresh herbs or essential oils.

To make herbal sachets and jars, mix dry herbs together and charge them with your intention. If the herbs are small enough, mix them as they are. If they are too big, use a mortar and pestle to grind them together. Place them in the container.

To close a sachet, tie it with a ribbon. To close a jar, seal it with wax from a candle. For the ribbon and the wax, use color correspondences to match your spell (page 142). Keep in mind that sachets and jars can also include other magickal items such as crystals, seashells, and symbols.

Herb Combinations for Sachets and Jar Spells

- Make a sachet with calendula and rosemary to give to the bride and the groom in handfasting ceremonies or weddings. It will promote an everlasting relationship.
- Create a sachet with chamomile, lavender, and rose quartz. Place it under your pillow to promote good sleep.
- Create a jar spell with salt, allspice, basil, and cinnamon. Use it to protect your home.

Potions

Herbal teas charged with your intent are called potions. This type of magick is a perfect way to combine the magickal and medicinal properties of herbs. There are many ways to charge them with your intent. These are two of the simplest methods.

Meditating: Make your tea and hold the cup in your projecting hand (page 30). Be careful not to burn yourself. It will be hot. Now focus on your goal and start sending your intention. Once you feel that the tea is charged, drink it.

Stirring: Make your tea. If you want to fulfill a goal, stir it clockwise to charge it with the intention. If you want to banish something, stir it counterclockwise to charge it with the intention.

You can charge the water that you use to brew your potions. Just place crystals near the water. Or try using moon water or sun water (page 159).

Recovery Potion

This is a potion that my mother showed me, and it is one of my favorites. It works wonders to speed your recovery from a sore throat or a mild cold.

Yield: 1 serving

2 teaspoons (2 g) thyme tea leaves
1 cup (240 ml) water charged with clear quartz
Juice of ½ lemon
1 teaspoon honey

Brew the thyme leaves in the water, then strain. Add the lemon juice. Pour in the honey and stir clockwise, focusing on healing.

The beauty of this potion is that it works even better if you brew it for someone else who is ill, as it will give them an extra boost of healing energy.

Other Uses for Herbs

Herbs are very versatile. If you are into them like me, you will find that they offer almost endless possibilities. Concoctions and salves can be used to help heal minor wounds and illnesses. Explore the benefits of herbs in your craft and experiment with other simple and effective uses for herbs in your life.

Herbs in Your Home

- Hang eucalyptus or lavender in your closet and place bay laurel leaves between your blankets when you store them. It will give them a pleasant smell and keep moths away.
- Keep pots with marigold and citronella on your windowsills to keep mosquitoes and other bugs away from your home.
- Use thyme to create a household cleaner. It is a natural disinfectant. Just mix the essential oil with natural soap and water.

Green Witchcraft and Kitchen Witchcraft

As you may have already realized, green witchcraft and kitchen witchcraft both draw on the power of herbs. There is a strong link between these two practices, and although not all green witches are kitchen witches and vice versa, they share quite a lot in common.

Some of the shared practices include growing herbs or spices, knowing their medicinal properties, and creating herbal teas, salves, and concoctions from scratch (rather than relying on store-bought).

Toxicity

Plants have compounds and chemicals that can react with your body and medications. Always ask your doctor before using or consuming an herb in any form to make sure that it is safe for you.

Essential oils must be diluted with a carrier oil before being used. Their strong properties can irritate and damage your skin if applied directly.

Some plants are toxic to animals, but not to humans. Please, research your plants and herbs before growing them. Think twice about what to plant in your garden if you have pets—or if you have pets in the neighborhood who visit your yard. In some cases, even eating a small part of a toxic plant can be fatal.

Things I Wish Someone Had Told Me

Smoke Cleansing vs. Smudging

Many people use smudging and smoke cleansing interchangeably, but they are not the same.

Smoke cleansing has been around since ancient times. It is a practice that is present across cultures, although the herbs vary as people used what grew where they lived. In witchcraft, we use different herbs, flowers, woods, and resins for cleansing. Smoke is an effective way to disrupt and eliminate unwanted energies (page 156). It is also a great technique for blessing, connecting with deities, and enhancing your psychic abilities.

Smudging is a tradition that originated with the indigenous tribes in North America. Smudging only uses white sage and is part of a complex ceremony. It has deeper meaning and the instructions for how to do it correctly are passed down within the community. Out of respect for Native American communities and their cultural traditions, do not appropriate the term *smudging*. Use *smoke cleansing* instead.

Herbs and Mother Earth

As our power comes from Mother Earth, our craft should be in tune with her. Plants and herbs are a big part of this special connection between witches and Nature.

Tips for Environmentally Friendly Witchcraft

- Use plants that grow where you live.
- Avoid plants that don't grow well in your zone.
- Avoid invasive plants.
- Plant species that help wild animals.
- Buy local herbs.
- If necessary, use natural pesticides and fertilizers.
- Avoid herbs that have been treated with unnecessary pesticides.

Traditional Medicine and Modern Medicine

Herbal remedies and other recipes from traditional medicine are not an alternative to or a substitute for modern medicine. For example, eating red berries is a great way to prevent urinary tract infections (UTIs), but if you contract one, you will need antibiotics as well. An untreated UTI can spread to the kidneys and become a life-threatening condition.

CHAPTER 7

DIVINATION

Many witches like to include divination as a part of their craft. When we tune in to our intuition—and sometimes use tools to channel it—we are able to access our higher self to find answers and guidance.

In this chapter, I talk about the senses that allow us to perceive these messages and the tools that allow us to focus and interpret them. Here you will discover your main clair sense as well as how to use tools like tarot, the pendulum or the runes to help you find answers to your questions. Keep in mind that divination is always subject to your interpretation, and it offers guidance more that straight forward answers. You and your actions are the ones that dictate your destiny.

Divination may seem like something that only gifted people can do. Whilst it's true that there are people born with certain skills, these skills can be trained. With an appropriated tool that resonates with you and practice, you can master divination. There is no one sense or tool that is superior to the rest. It is a matter of preferences and knowing when and how to use them.

The Eight Clair Senses

The clair senses are psychic senses that allow us to "feel" or predict something. They are strongly related to our intuition and gut feelings, and people usually feel a deeper connection with just one—but you can have more than one dominant clair sense.

Clairvoyance (Clear Seeing)

This is the most well-known clair sense. It is the ability to see images through your mind's eye. These extrasensory visions can take the form of mental images, symbols, colors, and more. Clairvoyants are able to see auras, spirits, faeries, and other types of energy. They also feel drawn to divination techniques that rely on seeing shapes, like scrying.

Do you present four or more of these traits?

- You are very visual and have good visual-spatial skills.
- You learn by watching others do things.
- You enjoy aesthetically pleasing images, rearranging things, and tidying spaces.
- You can quickly find coins, special pebbles, or lost items just with a quick glance.
- You can identify people with colors, or you see flashes of color with the corner of your eye when people walk by.

Claircognizance (Clear Knowing)

Claircognizants suddenly receive true information without having experienced something that leads them to that conclusion. Even without evidence, they are aware of facts that are revealed to them from an unknown source.

Becoming suddenly aware of something may trigger feelings or other sensations. With claircognizance, those emotions are caused *because of* the information and they are not *part of* the information.

Do you present four or more of these traits?

- You experience sudden moments of clarity.
- You prefer talking with a purpose and enjoy intellectual debates rather than small talk.
- You like experiencing new things.
- If you suddenly think about something or somebody, there is a high chance that you encounter them.
- You know what you want and are quick at making decisions.

Clairaudience (Clear Hearing)

People who are clairaudient perceive extrasensorial sounds, words, or noises. Those sounds don't come from a recognizable source; however, clairaudients can hear them clearly. The sounds usually provide important information that can trigger other thoughts.

Do you present four or more of these traits?

- You love music and singing, and you easily remember voices and rhythms.
- You learn quickly just by listening to somebody explaining things to you, and you easily remember things that people have told you.
- You enjoy paying attention to the sounds around you, sometimes focusing on one sound or conversation that doesn't involve you.
- What you usually remember the most from new experiences are the conversations.
- You enjoy working with music.

Clairsentience (Clear Feeling)

Clairsentience is one of the most common clair senses. It can be summed up as that gut feeling that is experienced viscerally. People who have this clair sense are called sentients. Clairsentience is linked to intuition, but sentients feel information physically.

Sentients experience all ranges of emotions and thoughts, but also physical feelings such as pain and pleasure. It takes practice to discern the emotions that a sentient can feel, and they are usually grouped into good or bad feelings. For a person who has just awakened their clairsentience, it can even be difficult to separate their own emotions from the ones that come from the outside.

Do you present four or more of these traits?

- Sometimes you experience feelings that are not related to your present situation. For example, having fun at a party and suddenly feeling sad out of nowhere.
- You tend to avoid crowded places.
- Your mood changes depending on who are you with. You are affected by their emotions.
- When someone you love is in pain, you feel pain as well.
- Your memories are often more related to your feelings than to physical experiences.

Clairtangency (Clear Touching)

Also known as psychometry, clairtangency is the ability to receive information about an item or a life being by touching. This clair sense is usually linked to others. This means that touching something or somebody is what triggers receiving knowledge, but the information is usually presented as sounds, images, smells, or other senses.

Do you present four or more of these traits?

- You learn faster by doing things yourself than you do by seeing how others do it or listening to them explain it to you.
- You prefer physical shopping over online shopping.
- You prefer firsthand objects, as the secondhand ones usually give you an odd feeling.
- Objects in museums always transmit some kind of energy to you.
- You can say whether the past owners of a house where happy or unhappy just by entering the house.

Clairalience (Clear Smelling)

A person with clairalience will receive information through smells without even using their physical nose. This means that even if you are breathing through your mouth, the smell will be clear and strong in your mind—and the people around who don't have this skill won't be able to smell it.

Some of the most common odors perceived are perfumes, food, and flowers. These smells are usually linked to events or people, triggering memories or other clair senses.

Do you present four or more of these traits?

- Sometimes smells trigger memories that you had forgotten.
- You remember clearly the perfume of people that you have just met, or it is usually the first thing you notice about them.
- You can identify spices, people, and places just by the smell.
- When you have a bad feeling about something, it is usually associated with an unpleasant smell.
- You know when it is going to rain because of a change in the smell of the air.

Clairgustance (Clear Tasting)

Having clairgustance means you suddenly taste something without any apparent reason. These flavors usually trigger other memories or clair senses. When a higher entity contacts us through clairgustance, it expresses a message through a flavor that you can relate to it.

The most common flavors recorded through clairgustance are food or beverages, but they can also be other substances, such as blood, if that would make the message clearer.

Do you present four or more of these traits?

- When you go on a trip, you can easily recall what you ate and whether you liked it or not.
- When you have a bad feeling about something, it is usually associated with an unpleasant taste or tasting blood.
- Flavors can easily trigger memories that you had forgotten.
- You can "taste smells."
- You get cravings that make you remember something.

Clairempathy (Clear Emotion)

People with clairempathy are called empaths. Empaths can sense emotions from other people: they don't need people to explain how they feel because they already know. The main difference between empaths and sentients is that while empaths sense an emotion or a thought, sentients feel and experience it. Empaths are some of the most sensitive people, and they need extra protection to avoid an energy overload.

Sometimes empaths are mistaken for highly sensitive people (HSP) and vice versa. Although many empaths are also HSP, they are not the same. An HSP processes a lot of information about their environment in shorter periods of time than most people, making them easily overwhelmed by interactions and other activities. However, they cannot feel other people's emotions.

Do you present four or more of these traits?

- You get easily overwhelmed when you are in crowded spaces or interact with many people.
- You can easily tell how a person is feeling and sometimes you confuse their feelings with your own.
- People usually seek your emotional advice, but you feel worn out after those kinds of interactions.
- You deeply dislike violent or tragic TV shows, books, and films.
- People feel calm when they talk to you, but you sometimes feel as though they have passed their worries to you.

Tarot

Cartomancy is fortune-telling using a deck of cards, and tarot is one of the most popular. Other forms of cartomancy use oracle decks or playing card decks.

The main difference between all these forms lies in the illustrations on the cards and their interpretation. A tarot deck has seventy-eight cards, twenty-two of them being major arcana and fifty-six being minor arcana. The major arcana are figures with symbolic meanings, and the minor arcana consists of four suits (pentacles, cups, wands, and swords) of fourteen cards each. The art of each tarot deck can vary depending on the artist, but the distribution and meaning of each card is the same.

Divination with playing cards also uses a fixed interpretation system for the usual four suits. With oracle decks, each creator decides which cards to incorporate and their meaning.

The number of the Fool often varies from one deck to another. This card, depending on the deck, can be the number 0, the number 22, or not have any number at all.

Interpreting the cards can be a tricky process. It is important to focus on each card and its relationship with other cards. A good reading helps you see the bigger picture.

MAJOR ARCANA	
0 The Fool	New beginnings, adventure, lack of discipline, exhibitionism
1 The Magician	Energy, motivation, willpower, fulfillment
2 The High Priestess	Intuition, esotericism, mystery, knowledge
3 The Empress	Motherhood, fertility, new ideas, art
4 The Emperor	Leadership, mundane knowledge, authority, rationality
5 The Hierophant	Traditions, old goals, constraints, wisdom
6 The Lovers	Optimism, contrasts, relationships, obsession
7 The Chariot	Overcoming obstacles, movement, changes
8 The Justice	Balance, justice, harmony, cause and effect
9 The Hermit	Secrets, austerity, potential, prudence
10 The Wheel of Fortune	Change, karma, cycles, destiny
11 The Strength	Valor, control, confidence, resolution
12 The Hanged Man	Slow down, reevaluate, effort, patience
13 The Death	Change, new beginnings, transformation, resignation
14 The Temperance	Harmony, moderation, stability, vital cycles
15 The Devil	Mistakes, unhealthy relationships, external forces, shadows
16 The Tower	Sudden changes, rebuilding, disturbance, moving forward
17 The Star	Renewal, hope, opportunities, meeting people
18 The Moon	Intuition, mental health, instability, illusions
19 The Sun	Abundance, success, happiness, vitality
20 The Judgment	Justice, evaluation, awakening, self-reflection
21 The World	Harmony, achievements, enlightenment, goals

Reading the cards is part of a larger ritual that involves cleansing and shuffling the cards. It is important to cleanse the cards in order to avoid any unwanted energy interfering with your reading and interpretations. I like burning a personal mix of herbs to cleanse the space and cards and to enhance my psychic abilities. By shuffling the cards, you imbue them with your energy and transmit the question that you need them to answer.

Once the deck is ready, start the reading. There are many different layouts for this. Choose the one that best suits your abilities or situation. Once you've decided the meaning of each position and drawn a card, it is very important to understand that you can't change it.

Two of the most common layouts are the Three Card Reading and the Celtic Cross.

Three Card Reading

Past/
Situation

Present/
Action

Future/
Outcome

Celtic Cross

Your Strength

Past

1

The Problem

Present

Root of the Problem

Future

Outcome

Advice

External Influences

How to Face It

Pendulum

Pendulums are great tools for self-discovery, energy detection, divination, and even contacting spirits. They usually consist of a pointy crystal attached to a rope or a chain. You can also find small silver chambers where you can burn herbs or incense. If you are on a budget, a necklace with a pointy crystal will work.

Start by cleansing the pendulum and the room. Hold the end of the chain with the thumb and middle finger of your projecting hand. Clear your mind and calibrate your pendulum. This is done by asking it to signal yes and then to signal no. The pendulum should rotate in one direction to signal yes and in the opposite to signal no. It can also react by drawing vertical and horizontal lines. Once it is calibrated, start the session by asking it yes/no questions.

To get more complex answers from a pendulum, use a pendulum chart. These divination boards have numbers, letters, or sentences written in them. Start in the center as a neutral position and let the pendulum choose its answer.

There are many other uses for pendulums. If you're looking for a lost object or a particular place, use a map to find it through its vibrations. If you carry a pendulum with you, you may be able to find places of high energy by paying attention to its reactions.

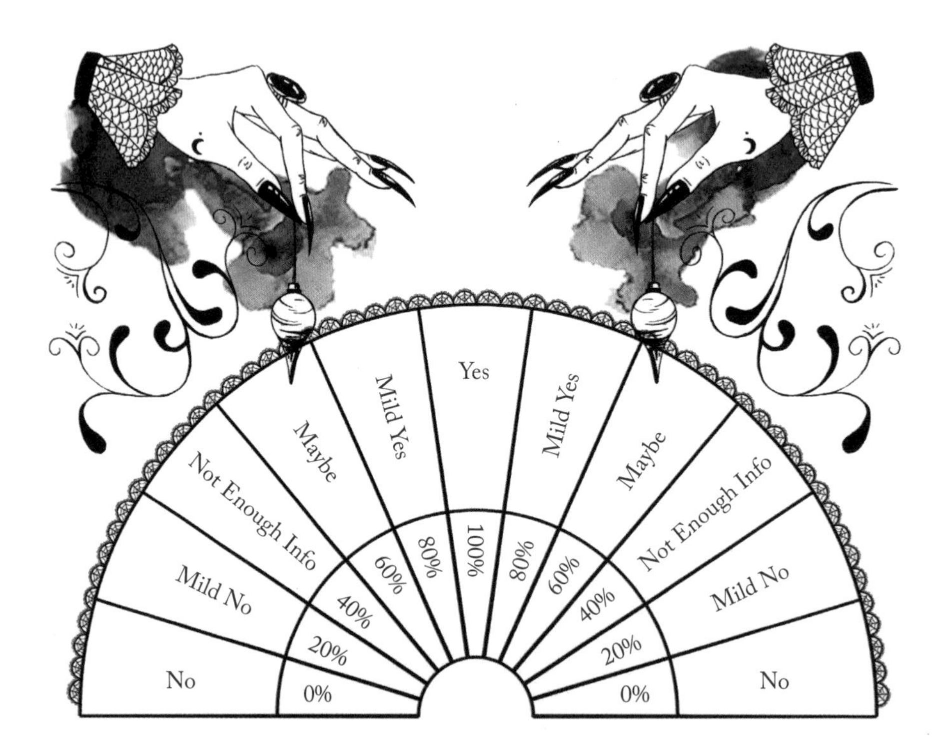

Runes

The runic alphabet is a writing system used by ancient Germanic and Proto-Norse languages. It was used as a writing method, but it is also a divination technique. Each symbol has an assigned meaning that transcends its letter nature.

The one that is most popular nowadays is the *Elder Futhark*. It is said that the runes were revealed to the Norse god Odin, who is known for seeking out knowledge to the point of obsession. To gain the wisdom needed to use the runes, Odin sacrificed himself by hanging himself from a sacred tree and piercing himself with a spear. He spent nine days like this without food or water. The runes accepted his offering and revealed themselves and their magickal uses to him. Odin became one of the most powerful gods in part due to the spells that he learned to cast with the runes.

The *Elder Futhark* consists of twenty-four runes equally divided into three families, or *aettir*, of eight runes. Each *aett* is dedicated to a deity: the first is the *aett* of the goddess Freya, the second is the *aett* of the god Heimdall, and the third is the *aett* of the god Tyr. The runes included in each *aett* are related to the traits of the deity that rules it. For example, Freya is associated with knowledge and creating, and all the runes included in her *aett* are related to those themes in one way or another. Some sets also include the black rune or the rune of Odin, a rune without inscription that was added in the twentieth century.

To use runes for divination, you can ask a simple question and take a rune from an opaque pouch. You can also use them in a similar way to tarot cards: choose a layout and pick a rune for each position. Lastly, you can throw them carefully and interpret their meaning, position, and relationship with the surrounding runes. It is important to use a rune cloth, a piece of fabric that will prevent the runes from getting damaged. Rune cloths can have designs on them that will help you interpret the place where the runes have landed.

Runes are a very versatile tool in witchcraft. As with tarot cards, you can use them in spells to reinforce the intention. You can carry one with you to manifest an aspect of that rune in your life, or you can meditate with one to try to achieve a revelation about that topic.

In addition to using runes to express intentions or realities, we can use them in combination (bind-runes) to express more complex concepts. We also use bind-runes as part of a ritual or to cast a spell. There are many common patterns and formulas for bind-runes that have been used successfully since ancient times.

You can also create your own bind-rune. To do this, first research your runes and make sure you understand how to use and read them. Overlay two or three simple runes that together express the intention that you have in mind. Try different compositions. Find the elements that overlap or that can be merged. Once you're happy with the design, charge it and use it the same way that you would a sigil (page 161). Don't forget to thank the runes for their guidance.

FREYA'S *AETT*: Duality, Creation, Love, and Education

Rune Name	Letter	Meaning
Fehu	F	Wealth, energy, fertility, good luck, abundance
Uruz	U	Strength, speed, desires, courage, inner energy
Thurisaz	TH	Change, overcoming obstacles, introspection
Ansuz	A	Communication, intelligence, inspiration, exams
Raido	R	Evolution, journeys, surprises, spiritual awakening
Kenaz	K/C	Knowledge, revelation, creativity, healing
Gebo	G	Gift, relationship, partnership, sacrifice
Wunjo	W	Joy, happiness, pleasure, good news

HEIMDALL'S *AETT*: Change, Mundane Activities, and Reflecting and Achievements

Rune Name	Letter	Meaning
Hagalaz	H	Change, obstacles, the forces of nature, destruction
Nauthiz	N	Necessity, sadness, patience, delays
Isa	I	Block, isolation, stillness, silence
Jera	J	Harvest, nature's cycles, rewards, closure
Eihwaz	Y	Strength, flexibility, ancestors, enlightenment
Perthro	P	Fortune, mystery, pawn, magick
Elhaz	Z	Protection, personal changes, friendship, self-defense
Sowilo	S	Health, success, energy, art/music

TYR'S *AETT*: Protection, Justice, and Divinity

Rune Name	Letter	Meaning
Tiwaz	T	Leadership, victory, honor, energy
Berkano	B	Fertility, new beginnings, patience, social skills
Ehwaz	E	Traveling, slow changes, new places, partnership
Mannaz	M	Mankind, culture, dignity, cooperation
Laguz	L	Flow, fertility, psychic skills, dreams
Ingwaz	NG	Fertility, relationships, family, common sense
Dagaz	D	Awareness, truth, clarity, surprise
Othala	O	Property, legacy, traditions, heritage

Scrying

Scrying is the practice of gazing into something, usually a reflective surface, to perceive images, words, or sensations. You open your inner psychic eye to see beyond mundane reflections. Eventually, visions will appear floating between your thoughts.

Practice is important to learn how to distinguish one vision from another. Some people are born with a natural ability to do this, but it is a skill that can take a lot of time and practice. The interpretation of those visions is up to you, and that also takes practice. Think of scrying as looking for shapes in the clouds. It takes a special vision to see them, and different people see different images.

The surface that you choose is something very personal. Some of the most common ones are mirrors and polished crystals (like crystal balls), but opaque crystals work too, especially if they distort the light. You can also incorporate nature in this ritual by trying water and fire scrying.

Dream Interpretation

Dreaming is such a common activity that often goes unnoticed. However, dreaming is essential for your body and mind, as it allows you to manage your emotions and create memories. A healthy sleep is one that includes dreams, even if we don't always remember them.

Some cultures consider dreams to be a portal to another dimension. Dreams are a way for our higher self to communicate. This communication takes place using symbols that take a shape that we can interpret. Thus, their meaning depends on our personal background and daily activities, and our culture and experiences deeply affect them. For example, dreaming about a dog won't have the same meaning for someone who has a beloved pet dog as it will to someone who was bitten by one.

The most important step in interpreting dreams—and one of the most difficult—is remembering them. One of the most effective ways is to write them down just as you wake up. Keep a notebook near your bed and write down everything you remember. Leave the interpretation for later. With time, you will start remembering dreams in more detail.

Dreams help us tune in to and connect our conscious and unconscious minds, preparing us for the challenges that we need to overcome. They allow us to connect with our occult skill. Sometimes you will see dreams or patterns that repeat themselves. This is a sign that something occupies your mind and you aren't taking proper care of it.

Sometimes you will realize mid-dreaming that you are, in fact, asleep and dreaming. This gives you the opportunity to explore lucid dreaming, which allows you to consciously delve into the land of the unconscious. This skill can also be trained, especially by suggestion. If you develop the habit of asking yourself "Am I dreaming?" while awake, you will start asking that to yourself while dreaming, triggering a lucid dream.

Carromancy

Carromancy is the interpretation of shapes in wax. All you need is a bowl with cold water and a candle. This works best if the color of the candle matches your intention. (See page 142 for color correspondences.)

A simple way to practice this divination technique is to find a quiet place where you can concentrate and not be disturbed. Fill a small bowl with cold water. A cereal bowl is perfect for this because it allows the wax drops to expand.

Hold your candle, take time to clear your mind, and then focus on your question. Light the candle and let the wax melt. Once there is a good amount of wax, drop it in the water. Try to drop the wax in the center of the bowl so it doesn't touch the walls and distort its shape.

The wax will create shapes on the surface for you to interpret. There are established meanings for some common shapes, but they can be very subjective. Let your intuition guide you.

Palmistry

Palmistry, also known as chiromancy, is the interpretation of the shape and lines of your hand to depict your personality and predict your future.

Before starting, choose which hand you are going to interpret. It is said that one hand expresses the future that you were born with, while the other expresses the future that you have created. There are two different traditions when it comes to deciding which hand matches which future. The first tradition says that a females' right hand is the one that you were born with, while the left one is how your actions have modified your path. For males, it would be the other way around. The second tradition, and the one I follow, says that your nondominant hand shows the destiny that you were assigned at birth, while the dominant hand shows the path that you have chosen. This is linked to the fact that using your hand will change the shape of its lines, so your nondominant hand is more likely to maintain a better representation of the lines that you had at birth.

Learning palmistry is a complex and long process, so here I'll only address the main aspects necessary for a global interpretation of the hand. There are three main aspects of the hand that you have to look for: lines, mounts, and shapes.

Lines

Lines are divided into major lines and secondary lines. The major lines give you an overall reading, while the secondary lines address the details. The three main lines in palm reading are the heart line, the head line, and the life line.

Heart Line

This is the line of relationships and love. The heart line is located closer to the fingers. It starts under the index finger or the middle finger and continues toward the pinky finger.

- If your heart line begins below the index finger, it means that you have a happy love life.
- If it begins below the middle finger, it means that you can be selfish in your relationships.
- A heart line that reaches both ends of the palm can mean dependency or lack of compromise.
- A short line means that you fall in love easily or that you prefer sexual relationships to love relationships.

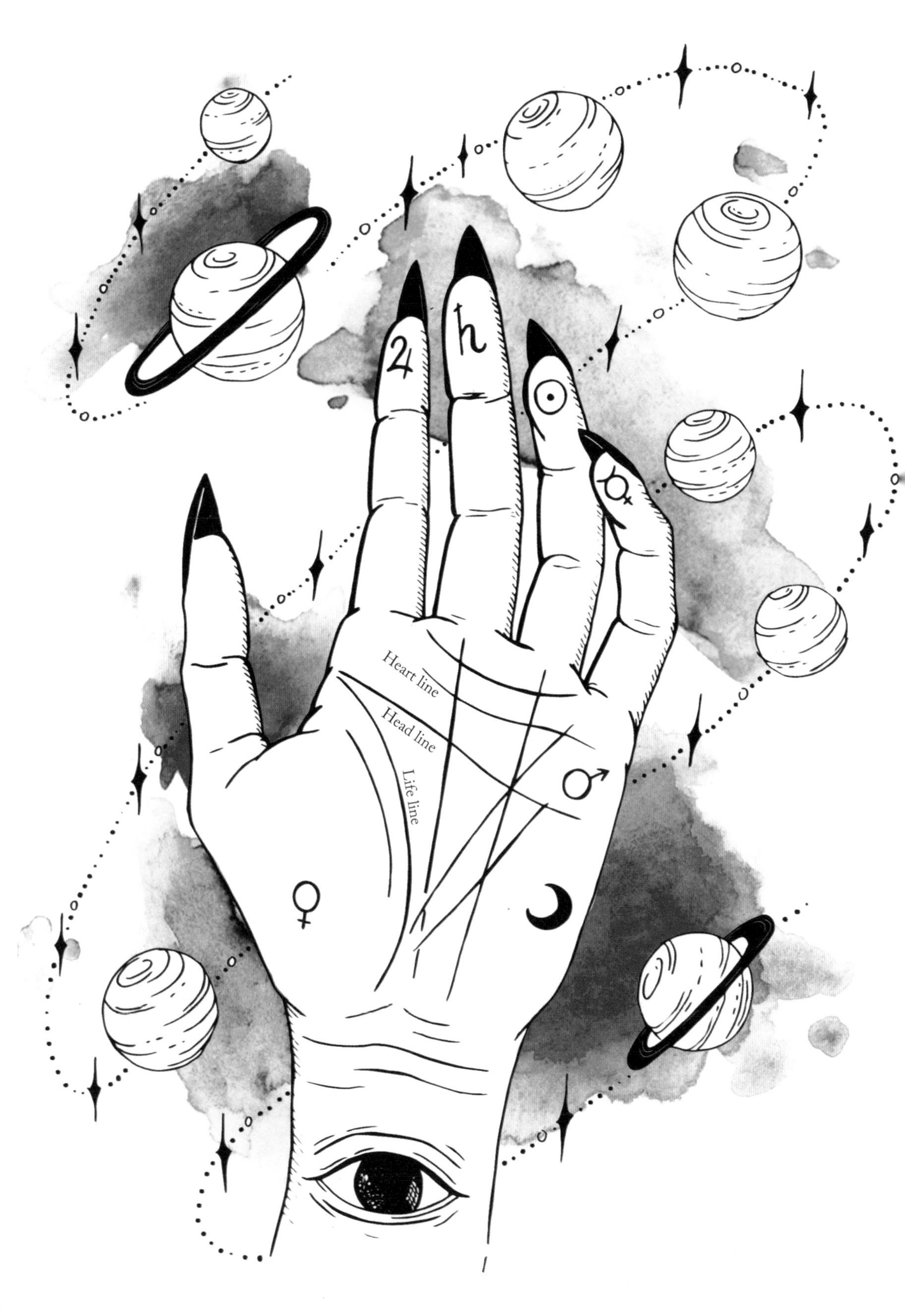
Heart line
Head line
Life line

- A straight line means that you don't pay much attention to love relationships or that you can easily control your emotions.
- A curved line shows that your emotions control you more than you control them.
- A wavy line indicates an absence of serious relationships.
- If there are circles, the line is broken, or smaller lines cross it, it indicates trauma and sadness.

Head Line

The head line starts between the index finger and the thumb. It is located between the heart line and the life line, in the middle of the palm, crossing it. This line is related to mental and thought processes as well as intelligence.

- A long line denotes good memory and intelligence. The longer the line is, the better these attributes are.
- A straight line shows calmness and knowing how to manage your emotions.
- A curved line is a sign of creative and idealistic people.
- A broken line indicates indecisiveness and nervousness.
- A line that is crossed by smaller lines indicates very important decisions.
- A line that is branched upward signifies academic success, while a line branched downward signifies mental illness.
- A deep line denotes a clear, focused mind and concise thinking.
- A wavy line is a sign of instability or a short attention span.

Life Line

The life line starts under the head line and creates an arc around the thumb, extending to almost reach the wrist. This line is related to the length of the life itself as well as lifestyle and life choices.

- A deep line indicates a healthy life and vitality, while a fainter one usually indicates health problems.
- A line that is close to the thumb, especially if it is short, denotes limited energy.
- Multiple life lines show that you have friends or family who will help you through life.
- If the line breaks and starts another line, it is a sign of a sudden change in lifestyle: either positive or negative.
- A semicircular line around the thumb line shows enthusiasm and vigor.
- Short lines crossing the life line represent sudden dangers or misfortunes.
- A circle in the line shows injuries or illnesses. If the whole line looks "chained," it is a sign of poor health since birth.
- Several branches in the life line indicate multiple paths.

Mounts

The mounts are the bumps of flesh on the palm. They are part of advanced palmistry and usually have an important role in palm reading. Each mount is named after a celestial body and is linked to a life aspect related to that celestial body.

Examine its shape: Is it raised? Is it flat? Is it merged with other mounts? Look for markings, such as chains or stars. A well-developed mount shows that the characteristics related to it have an important place in the life of that person. A normal mount is in proportion to the other mounts and to the hand as a whole, and a flat or absent mount is a sign of lack of that personal trait.

There are nine mounts in total. Looking at your left hand, from left to right and top to bottom, they are the following.

Mount of Jupiter

Located at the base of the index finger, it represents willpower, authority, and ambition. If it is well developed, it shows that you are reliable. If it is overdeveloped (higher than the rest), it can be a sign of possessiveness and lack of compassion. A soft mount of Jupiter is usually a sign of overindulgence, and a flat or absent mount of Jupiter shows lack of self-esteem or ambition.

Mount of Saturn

You will find this mount at the base of your middle finger. It is the mount of discipline and responsibility. A well-developed mount of Saturn indicates intelligence, responsibility, and independence. If it is overdeveloped, it shows a tendency for cynical thinking and isolation. A flat mount of Saturn shows a strong faith in fate or other superstitions or religious systems. People with flat or absent mounts of Saturn are scrupulous but can be saddened easily.

Mount of the Sun

Also called the mount of Apollo, this is the mount of creativity, wealth, and influence. It is located at the base of the ring finger. A well-developed mount shows love for the arts, compassion, and flexibility to changes. If it is overdeveloped, it can be a sign of envy and a hot temper. If it is flat or it does not appear, it can indicate a poor aesthetic taste, difficulty standing out in a crowd, and poor decision-making skills.

Mount of Mercury

Located at the base of the pinky finger, the mount of Mercury is associated with communication, thinking processes, and wisdom. A well-developed mount is a trait of resourceful people. If it is overdeveloped, it shows that you tend to talk too much or be insincere. If it is flat or absent, it can show shyness or an inability to communicate with others.

Inner/Lower Mount of Mars

This mount is located at the side of the palm, between the mounts of Jupiter and Venus. If it is well developed, it shows courage, but if it is overdeveloped, it shows aggressiveness. A low or absent inner mount of Mars is a sign of uncertainty and self-consciousness.

Plain of Mars

Located in the center of the palm, the plain of Mars is not technically a mount, so the interpretation is a bit different. A well-defined plain shows a confident and balanced person. A low plain is a sign of easily influenced people.

Outer/Upper Mount of Mars

This mount is located on the side of the palm, between the heart line and the head line. It represents self-control and temperament. A well-developed mount is a sign of strong will and perseverance. An overdeveloped mount shows a lack of fear of danger, and a flat mount shows a lack of perseverance or an inability to express feelings.

Mount of Venus

This mount is located at the base of the thumb and is surrounded by the life line. This mount represents love and affection. If it is well developed, it shows a balanced, sensual, and affectionate person. If it is overdeveloped, it is a sign of an overindulgent person who is highly influenced by family and traditions. If it is low or absent, it is typically a sign of a coldhearted person with weak family bonds.

Mount of the Moon

Also called the mount of Luna, this mount is located at the opposite side of the mount of Venus. This mount is related to creativity, intuition, and emotions. A prominent mount represents a person with a highly developed intuition, imagination, and psychic abilities. If it is overdeveloped, it is a sign of a sentimental person who tends to fantasize to the point of being absent. A low mount represents a lack of new ideas.

Shapes

Studying the shape of the hand is called chirognomy, and it is a discipline of its own. It is an offshoot of palmistry, and many palmists use it to create a more holistic interpretation of the palm. Chirognomy interprets the shape and size of the hand, fingers, and nails; the texture and flexibility of the skin; and the presence or absence of hair, among other features.

When studying the shape of the hand, there are two approaches. The first branch classifies seven types of hands: square, spatulate, conical, knotty, pointed, elemental, and mixed. The second branch classifies hands by assigning them an element. The Chinese palmistry tradition uses the elements earth, fire, air, water, wood, and metal. The Western palmistry tradition, which is the one explained below, uses air, fire, water, and earth.

Air

Air hands have long, bony fingers with a shorter, usually square, palm. People who have this kind of hand are usually very mentally active, thus easily bored. They are always looking for new challenges and they solve problems in their own way. Although they have good instincts, they are very logical and like to analyze the details. Because of this, they can be perceived as cold, although they tend to be sociable and talkative. They need the right amount of stimulation or they can become anxious.

Fire

Fire hands have a long, rectangular palm with shorter fingers. Most people with this kind of hand are outgoing and extroverted. They are usually enthusiastic and optimistic, but this can easily turn into impulsiveness and egoism. They are passionate and confident in their abilities, and are led by their heart and desires, even if this brings them problems. As the life of the party, they always make fun companions, but they can also be very impatient. They need to pay attention to the signs of burnout, as it can easily happen to them.

Water

Water hands have long palms and long fingers. They are usually shaped like an oval and tend to have soft skin. This kind of hand is linked to introverted people who are really in tune with their intuition. Psychic abilities are something natural for them. They are very creative, especially in calm and quiet environments. Their decisions are ruled by their heart and feelings, making them perceived as moody or thin-skinned. They are particularly sensitive to negative emotions, such as sadness or stress.

Earth

Earth hands have short palms and short fingers. They are squared and broad, usually with a thick skin. People with earth hands tend to be hardworking and have solid values to the point of sometimes being stubborn. They have a practical and realistic point of view and are reliable and stable. Although they are responsible, they can be short-tempered and materialistic at times. They enjoy manual work and being outdoors in contact with nature.

Some palmists who use this approach like to complete their interpretation with astrology, linking the element of the hand with the element of the zodiac sign.

Things I Wish Someone Had Told Me

Divination Is for Advice

You are the master of your fate, and your decisions in the present can and will change the future. As with dream interpretation, there are established meanings to guide your interpretation—but you also need to interpret them through the lens of your personal experiences. The first interpretation that comes to your mind is the right one. Your intuition will guide you if you are honest with yourself.

It is also important to keep in mind that you should not base all your decisions on divination. It is a powerful tool that can provide insight into your personal situation, but you also need to be able to make decisions on your own.

Bond with Your Divination Tools

To obtain accurate answers to your questions, create a bond with your divination tools. When you use a pendulum, cards, or runes, you are what gives them power. Divination tools serve as a focal point to channel the information that *your* subconscious perceives. This is why it is important to create a bond. Think of your divination tools as the ship that allows you to sail the seas of your subconscious or acts as an antenna to receive messages that may have gone unnoticed. The more you know your tools, their reactions and sensibilities, and the stronger your bond is, the better your divination skills will become.

Ways to Bond with Your Divination Tools

- Carry them with you to transmit your energy to them.
- Place them under your pillow or near your bed while you sleep.
- Study their shape, artwork, and meanings.
- Keep a divination journal.
- Ask them a quick and simple question every day.
- For decks, shuffle them.

Bonding is something very personal, so choose or create a method that you prefer.

Runes and Cards for Spells

Runes and cards can be used to reinforce the effect of a spell if their meaning matches your intention. They can also be used as offerings or altar decorations, or you can incorporate them into meditations with a set goal.

CHAPTER 8

Working with Spirits and Deities

There are different realms separated from our mundane world. Witches can access and work with the entities that inhabit them, and these entities can also reach us. If you decide to incorporate them into your craft, it's important to keep in mind that they have their own personality and you will be working together.

This part of the craft is probably one of the most personal and intimate ones. The relationship that you establish with deities and other entities is completely unique. As we grow older and our life changes, so do we. Because of this, don't be afraid to search for new relationships or change the ones that you already have with deities and spirits. Different life stages have different needs and wants.

In this chapter, we will explore the spirit realm, including how to honor your ancestors and how to be safe when contacting spirits. I also give some notions about how to work with deities, as well as mention ten of the most popular ones between Western witches. Of course, there are many other deities from different cultures that you can explore, depending on your traditions, cultural background, and type of witchcraft.

The Spirit Realm

As we saw in the first chapter, witchcraft is not linked to any belief system. It is a practice, not a religion. Most witches believe in the existence of a different realm inhabited by spirits. However, there are many points of view about how the spirit world works.

Usually the spirit world is defined as a realm in which spirits and other entities made from energy reside. The communication channels are not always open between worlds, at least for us. Some entities are able to open portals on their own. To contact their dimension, we usually need some kind of tool, although if we share a deep bond with the spirit we may be able to communicate without any assistance.

For witches who believe in reincarnation, the spirit realm is seen as a step for human souls before starting a new life. Some souls spend more time in it than others. It is also a common belief that human souls share the spirit world with other entities, such as familiars (page 138).

Some witches believe that these other entities have their own domain. For example, the realm of the faeries is considered a parallel dimension: They share the same physical space as us, but their spirits are in a different place. They can cross over to our realm and intervene in it, but usually we cannot see them unless we have the right tools or they allow it.

During certain dates, such as Samhain and Beltane (pages 70 and 58), the division between worlds decreases, and it is easier to establish contact with the other side. This event is usually referred to as the "thinning veil."

Contacting Spirits Safely

Spirits and entities are not always friendly, and you must be careful. If you decide to contact a spirit, participate in séances with more experienced witches before trying to do one on your own. When contacting spirits, you need to learn to recognize signals that indicate you should dismiss the spirit and close the session.

These are some of the signs of not-so-friendly spirits:

- They are impatient or aggressive. They may even threaten you physically or in other ways. The spirit may try to persuade you to do things, telling you that you aren't choosing the right path or that bad things may happen.
- They don't respect your free will and try to persuade you to do things for them, telling you that you are the only one who can.

- They talk about secrets, ancient magick, and portals, but they never give you useful information.
- They tell you that you are very special and that you are the only one whom they have contacted and who can channel their powers.
- They try to isolate you from your family or friends, saying that they want to protect you.

If you experience some of these red flags, or you simply get an uneasy feeling when contacting that spirit, dismiss them and cleanse your home (page 156).

Honoring the Dead

Honoring your ancestors is a long-standing practice both within and outside of witchcraft. It allows us to remember our loved ones who have passed away and seek guidance from those in the spirit world. If you want to honor a particular person, the rituals may be customized by including photos, personal possessions, and things that the person liked.

These are some ideas that can be adapted to almost everybody:

CREATE AN ANCESTOR ALTAR Use this space to remember one or several of your loved ones. As with every altar, it is a workspace where you can work with your energy and the energy of your ancestors. It usually includes a small space for offerings, although some witches prefer to pray instead.

GIVE OFFERINGS Place objects or food the person you are remembering would have enjoyed on your altar. One of the most popular ones is brewing tea and sharing it with an ancestor. This practice is similar to Samhain's dumb supper (page 72). It doesn't need to be a specific blend, just something they would have enjoyed. Actions can also be offerings, so do something good in their honor.

KEEP THEIR MEMORY ALIVE Tell stories about them, look at photos of them, and visit their grave. Enjoy a relaxing moment at the altar thinking about the memories that you have of them. This should not be a sad moment, but more of an uplifting one.

RESEARCH YOUR FAMILY LINEAGE Rediscover those who are part of your family's past but who have been forgotten.

COMMUNICATE WITH THEM Write a letter to them and burn it at your altar. Send them prayers or ask for their help in a craft that they were skilled at. This will help you create and maintain stronger bonds.

Deities

Some witches channel their spirituality through deities, establishing a very personal relationship. Deities are a higher power, but at the same time they are our companions. They allow us to access the higher power inside ourselves that they embody. Nevertheless, there are witches who don't worship deities because they prefer to obtain their power from other sources.

Depending on culture, tradition, and personal preferences, some witches feel more drawn to some deities than others. The set of deities that are worshiped in a determinate religion or tradition are normally called a pantheon. The pantheon worshiped by a person is something very intimate because the connection that is established with deities is strong. When choosing the deities that you want to worship, it is said that you don't find the right gods; they find you. This means that you should feel a calling from them and possibly experience signals. You can find signs that a deity is calling you in your daily life, meditation, or dreams.

Your pantheon may change over time. As we experience life, we feel more drawn to deities that match our needs and beliefs at that stage of our path. Some pagans build a special relationship with a god or a goddess that takes the main place in their belief system. These deities are called patron or matron deities.

There are many deities, and their action fields differ. Because of this, when asking for power for a specific matter, we should ask the right deity. If our request falls outside a deity's scope, they most likely won't be able to help us. For example, if your goal is love related, Venus, goddess of love, would be an appropriate deity—not Ares, god of war.

Research deities before you start to worship them. Deities' correspondences and action fields sometimes overlap, and a better understanding of their power will provide you with better results. When you work with a deity, it is important to bear in mind that you work together. Deities may grant you their help, but you need to work for your goals as well. Sometimes a deity may adapt to your personal situation and see further than you can, helping you achieve what you need in that moment.

Here are ten of the most commonly worshiped gods and goddesses from different pagan religions. There are many others. Explore and find the one that resonates with you.

Athena

Renamed Minerva by the ancient Romans, Athena is the Greek goddess of wisdom, science, art, creativity, and handicraft. She is also goddess of strategy and war, joining intuition with planning and avoiding unnecessary violence in war. She helped several heroes in their missions and never took any lovers. Athena is usually represented as an owl, and this association has carried through to today, making owls a symbol of wisdom.

Bastet (Bast or Baset)

This ancient Egyptian goddess is the defender of the sun god, Ra. She is also the protector of women, children, and childbirth. She is the goddess of festivals, music, dance, and fertility. At first, she was depicted as a lioness warrior, but her image changed with time to the cat goddess. Because of this, all cats are sacred to Bastet.

Belenus (Belinus)

Among the Celts, Belenus is god of the sun, fire, and light. His name means "the shining one." He is usually depicted accompanied by a goddess named Belisama with whom he shared some sun attributes, although she had her own correspondences as well.

Brigit (Brigid)

Brigit is the Celtic goddess of fire. She is related to the return of the spring, and the sabbat Imbolc is dedicated to her (page 52). Brigit protects women, children, and newborn babies and animals. She is associated with healing, poetry, and blacksmith's work and is conceived as the embodiment of the higher state of the mind. She is known as the triple goddess and is sometimes represented as three women.

Cernunnos

This horned god is the Celtic deity of the environment and, in particular, of forests. He is a protector and the embodiment of regeneration; his emotions and actions control the cycles of nature. During Beltane fertility dances (page 60), men dress as Cernunnos to welcome the fertility of the soil and the animals. He is usually represented as a man with antlers, seated with his legs crossed, but as he changes with the seasons he can also be represented as an old man.

Freya (Freyja)

Traveling in a cat-drawn chariot, Freya is the Norse goddess of love and fertility and also of war and death. She rules a heavenly field named Fólkvangr, where she receives half of those who died in combat (the other half go to Odin's field, Valhalla). Freya also receives women who have suffered a noble death. She is usually depicted with the Brísingamen, a golden necklace that represents the origin of life.

Hades

Hades and his two brother, Zeus and Poseidon, defeated their father and the rest of the Titans to become the new rulers of the universe. They divided it in three parts, and Hades received the underworld. He is described as mostly calm and passive, rarely leaving the underworld, except when someone tries to break his rules, in which case he punishes them severely. The ancient Romans renamed him Pluto. He is often represented with his three-headed dog, Cerberus.

Hekate (Hecate)

This Greek goddess is the mother of witches. She holds the ancient knowledge of witchcraft, herbal medicine, poisons, and necromancy. She is usually seen as a matron, taking care of the household. She is the one who helps us be born, but also the one who helps us die and go to the other side. She is represented as three people or with three heads. Dogs are sacred to Hekate, and she is usually depicted along with a friendly female dog, but she can also be accompanied by nocturnal animals.

Loki

The trickster god Loki is one of the most popular Norse gods. He is a shape-shifter and appears in mythology as a mare and a salmon, among other shapes. He is very intelligent, but he is also mischievous, sometimes helping the rest of the gods and other times tricking them. Because of his acts against the gods, he is condemned to be tied up in a cave while venom from a snake drips over him. His wife gathers the venom in a bowl, but when she needs to empty it, the poison falls on Loki and his screams create earthquakes.

Osiris

The Egyptian god of resurrection has a bittersweet story. He was killed by his brother, but his wife, Isis, found his body and revived him, allowing him to conceive his son, Horus, posthumously. He is also strongly related to wheat because wheat germinates and dies, only to germinate again. Osiris rules the underworld. He is usually depicted as a man with green skin, with his body or part of it mummified, and he carries symbols of pharaohs. He was one of the most worshiped gods in ancient Egypt, and he still has great popularity in the pagan community.

Things I Wish Someone Had Told Me

How to Meet Your Familiar

Familiars are a type of spirit present in several pagan traditions. They are usually defined as low-ranking sprits or demons that help witches in their craft, but they can also be seen as a projection of ourselves. They help witches access information or places that we can't reach, and they guide us on our path.

Familiars are shape-shifters. They can adopt different appearances, but one of the most common is as animals. It is important to make a distinction between pets and familiars. Although familiars can appear as pets, not all pets are familiars and vice versa. If you want to know whether your pet is also your familiar, ask yourself whether it helps you in your craft.

If you are trying to find your familiar, be patient and receptive. Your familiar will appear when you are ready, and it can do so in any shape. Listen to your intuition. Do you feel a special and spiritual affinity with some type of animal? If you are having difficulty finding it, try meditation or lucid dreaming (page 121) to contact its spirit and ask it for its help.

Oil

CHAPTER 9

Correspondences, Rituals, and Spells

Correspondences are the magickal properties linked to objects, times, and planets, among other things. They play an important role in the symbolism behind rituals, and using them well can increase your spell's probability of success.

For me, witchcraft is a celebration. I like to approach my craft in a cheerful way. My spirituality is how I celebrate life and nature. Because of this, all the correspondences I use are a way to a way to tune in with the natural elements and cycles of the Universe. However, correspondences are usually affected by cultural background, keep in mind that you should feel that they are aligned with your intention.

In this chapter, we see how correspondences work. You will find tables and explanations for different elements of rituals and spells such as colors, materials and timing. Then we turn to some essential practices —such as cleansing and charging— as well as a few fundamental spells and rituals that can be incorporated by any type of witch to their craft.

Correspondences

In witchcraft, choosing the correct ingredients with the correct correspondences to perform a ritual or spell will boost its energy. We have already discussed how crystals and herbs have correspondences (see chapters 5 and 6, respectively). In this section, we take a more in-depth look at correspondences and their general application to witchcraft.

Colors

Colors have strong symbolism in witchcraft. This belief is rooted in the science behind colors. Each color absorbs and reflects a determinate wavelength of light. For example, if something is red, that means that it is absorbing all the wavelengths except for the red one, which is reflected and reaches our eyes. Different wavelengths have different properties, and so do colors. One of the easiest ways to observe this phenomenon is by comparing white and black objects. White reflects all the wavelengths while black absorbs all of them, causing black objects to heat faster than white ones.

Here are the correspondences usually associated with each color. However, they may vary from one tradition to another. Color correspondences can be applied to clothes, candles, sigils, talismans, or anything that you can think of. Some colors are connected with the five elements, and the combination of all of them, the rainbow, represents the connection between the earth and the sky.

Flames

When you cast a spell that involves candles, don't forget to watch the flames. Their shape and intensity will give you clues about its final outcome. Be sure to look for mundane reasons for why the flame may be behaving in a particular way.

Wood

Items such as wands and altar plates can be made from different materials. One of the most traditional is wood. Wood is also a central part of some sabbats, being used to make the Yule log (page 51) or different bonfires.

The correspondences of each tree come from the Celtic tree calendar, an ancient moon calendar with thirteen divisions that assigns one tree to each month. Although it is called Celtic, historians disagree as to whether the ancient Celts used it. Other types of wood have correspondences that have been assigned to them later as well.

COLOR	CORRESPONDENCES
White	Purity, truth, innocence, initiation
Black	Challenges, protection, prohibition, defense (If used with white, it signifies balance and opposites.)
Violet	Spirituality, wisdom, clairvoyance, psychic powers
Blue	Calm, healing, dreams, intuition
Green	Fertility, abundance, rebirth, good luck
Yellow	Communication, creativity, learning, imagination
Orange	Happiness, opportunities, strength, vitality
Red	Courage, power, love/passion, danger
Pink	Romance, friendship, children, compassion
Brown	Stability, material goods, decision making, home

TYPE OF FLAME	MEANING
Strong Flame	Your intention is robust and the spell will be too. It represents strong feelings, such as love or anger.
Weak Flame	You are facing a heavy opposition, or your intention is not strong enough.
Dancing Flame	Your energy is erratic. Challenges or changes are approaching.
Flickering Flame	Sprits are present.

Here are the correspondences for the wood of each tree of the Celtic tree calendar. Although reed does not have wood, I decided to include it because it is part of the Celtic tree calendar, and it can be used to make items, such as wind instruments, or it can be burned.

TREE	CORRESPONDENCES
Birch	Fertility, creativity, new beginnings
Rowan	Protection, the dead, initiation
Ash	Magick, knowledge, spirituality, faerie protection
Alder	Divination, intuition, faerie magick
Willow	Protection, healing, the dead, knowledge, female energy
Hawthorn	Making decisions, defense, cleansing, contacting faeries, male energy
Oak	Power, leadership, wealth, luck, strength
Holly	Protection against spirts, rebirth
Hazel	Knowledge, dream interpretation, fertility, safe traveling
Vine	Prosperity, joy, strong emotions
Ivy	Banishing, cleansing, protection, healing
Reed	Meditation, grounding, energy work, honoring the dead, rebirth
Elder	Creativity, protection against negative spirits, connecting with Mother Earth (The Wiccan tradition advises not to burn elder in order to avoid negative energies.)

Timing

There are cycles in the Earth that are repeated periodically. Most pagans and witches celebrate these cycles and learn from them, as with the eight sabbats that revolve around the cycle of seasons.

Waiting for the right moment to cast a spell or a ritual will help you boost its efficiency. Some traditions give more importance to timing than others. If you depend on the energy of the universe to cast spells, timing may be a decisive factor in the outcome. If you use your own inner energy, timing is important but not essential; timing may make your spells more powerful, but, usually, it is not a reason for them to fail or backfire.

Some of the most common timing correspondences are days of the week, hours of the day, astrological/astronomical events, and moon phases. Sometimes not all of these correspondences match up, so you need to prioritize one over the rest. This decision depends on your tradition, skills, and abilities, but one of the most popular among witches are moon phases and astronomical/astrological events, as their energy is easily felt.

Days of the Week

Each day of the week is consecrated to an ancient Greek/Roman deity and consequently to the planet that is named after that deity and its correspondences.

	MONDAY	TUESDAY	WEDNESDAY	THURSDAY	FRIDAY	SATURDAY	SUNDAY
Deity (Greek/ Roman)	Selene/ Luna	Ares/ Mars	Hermes/ Mercury	Zeus/ Jupiter	Aphrodite/ Venus	Cronus/ Saturn	Apollo/ Sol
Planet	Moon	Mars	Mercury	Jupiter	Venus	Saturn	Sun
Correspon-dences	Dreams, intuition, fertility, wisdom	Courage, strength, protection, success	Commu-nication, learning, memory, traveling	Prosperity, wealth, luck	Love, beauty, seduction, art	Banishing, cleansing, discipline, change	Health, happiness, growth, joy

Planetary Influences

Astrology is a complex field with its own terminology, and my advice is to consult specialized sources. It is also a good idea to obtain a basic understanding of astronomy, particularly the positions of the celestial bodies in the sky. Keep in mind that the astrology discussed in this book is Western astrology; the stars have different meanings in other cultures.

Some witches, mostly cosmic witches, like to synchronize their rituals with astrological events. The most common ones are the zodiac seasons (the period of the year ruled by a zodiac sign), planetary hours, and the position and motion of celestial bodies.

Birth Charts

A birth chart is a report of the astrological energies at the moment when you were born. It considers the placement of the celestial bodies, taking into account the day, the hour, and the place where you were born.

Birth charts have three main components:

HOUSES These are the twelve main divisions of the birth chart. They represent the path of the planets in the sky from the Earth. Because they show static places, they are always in the same position on birth charts. The left side is the east or ascendant, and the houses start from there in counterclockwise order. The right side is named the descendant. This division means that the upper half of the chart is the sky over the horizon, and the lower half is the sky under the horizon. Depending on the astrological tradition, the houses may or may not be the same length. Each house represents an area of our lives.

ZODIACS SIGNS These signs correspond to where the zodiac was placed in the sky at the moment of birth. These divisions are mobile and change depending on the time of the year, and they are not the same for everybody. Each sign has particular personality traits.

PLANETS OR CELESTIAL BODIES Each planet has different connotations and correspondences. When you are born, the planets are in a determinate place in their orbit and thus our night sky. We can interpret personality based on the position of the planets in relation to the houses and zodiac sign.

Understanding a Birth Chart

Here are three main aspects that we look for in a birth chart.

SUN The placement of the sun represents your personality. The sun zodiac is the sign that is commonly known as your "zodiac sign" and is used for less complex horoscopes.

MOON The placement of the moon in your birth chart reflects your inner world and personality.

ASCENDANT SIGN To find out your ascendant sign, check the zodiac sign that was in the ascendant part of the house chart. It will give you information about how your life will unfold. This is determined by the ascendant, as well as how other people perceive you. But, as with everything related to divination or astrology, you can change it through your actions and effort.

Your birth chart helps you know yourself better and tune in to your craft with what the stars say of you.

ZODIAC SIGN	DATES*	CORRESPONDENCES
Aries	March 21–April 20	A new zodiac year is starting. It will bring new beginnings, new projects, and lots of energy.
Taurus	April 21–May 21	Taurus brings steady energy, perfect to keep working on your projects. It also brings luxurious and sensual energy to take a break from work.
Gemini	May 22–June 21	Winds of change come with Gemini. Your head will be buzzing with ideas. It is a good moment to socialize.
Cancer	June 22–July 22	Cancer is a call to let your heart guide you and surround yourself with your loved ones.
Leo	July 23–August 22	Leo brings a confident and carefree mind-set. It is time to just enjoy being yourself.
Virgo	August 23–September 22	During Virgo season, it is time to ground yourself and plan your next steps. Take care of your mind and body.
Libra	September 23–October 22	Libra means balance and harmony; however, pursuing those in excess may make you too sensitive.
Scorpio	October 23–November 22	Scorpio is a time to engage in spiritual renewal. Tune in to your intuition and discover the raw truth.
Sagittarius	November 23–December 21	Sagittarius season is a time to be open-minded and flexible. Leave your comfort zone and try new things.
Capricorn	December 22–January 20	This season calls you to ground yourself and meditate. Being present will help you enjoy the moment.
Aquarius	January 21–February 19	The Aquarius season is the perfect moment to let your imagination fly and think about the future.
Pisces	February 20–March 20	During Pisces season, you will be called to follow your intuition and be empathetic with other people.

* There may be changes depending on the astrological tradition.

Zodiac Seasons

Zodiac seasons, planetary hours, and planet placements are also ways to tune in to your craft. The zodiac seasons divide the astrological year into the twelve zodiacs, creating the zodiac wheel. The dates of the seasons are the ones for the regular horoscope or the sun sign; because of this, they are also called solar seasons. Each sign has particular aptitudes and correspondences that affect that period of time.

Each season interacts differently with each zodiac sign. This means that, even if the overall energy is the same, a Scorpio season may affect a person with sun sign Libra differently than it will someone with sun sign Leo.

Planetary Hours

Planetary hours are not as popular as they used to be, but there are witches who still follow them. Each planetary hour is linked to a celestial body. There are twelve planetary hours in total, and they are calculated from sunrise to sundown, so they don't have sixty minutes and vary from one day to another.

I use a pretty simple method to calculate them. However, there are more exact and difficult ones.

- The day is divided into daytime and nighttime. Daytime begins from the exact hour of sunrise to the exact hour of sundown. The same goes for nighttime, from sundown to sunrise.
- Choose whether you will perform your ritual during day or night and calculate the exact number of minutes that it lasts.
- Divide that number of minutes equally among the twelve planetary hours. That is the duration of a day hour or night hour.
- Now is when it may get a bit tricky. Check the date for when you want to perform the ritual and the planet that rules that day of the week (page 145). Because you have already chosen whether you want to cast it in the first twelve hours or second twelve hours of the day, you only need to assign a celestial body to those twelve hours (and not the twenty-four hours of the day). The first day/night hour will be the one that corresponds with the day. Then you just need to repeat the same sequence: Venus ☞ Mercury ☞ Moon ☞ Saturn ☞ Jupiter ☞ Mars ☞ Sun.
- The correspondences for each planet are the same as the ones described in the table of the days of the week (page 145).

To simplify it a bit, let's try an example. Say we want to cast a spell for self-love, but we can only cast it on a Sunday, so we want to find the Venus hour because Venus is the appropriate planet for this matter.

- We want to cast the spell during daytime. The sunrise is at 8:36 a.m., and sunset is at 7:00 p.m. If we calculate the daytime that we have, we get 10 hours and 24 minutes, or 624 minutes.
- If we divide 624 minutes by the 12 hours, we get that every day hour lasts 52 minutes.
- Because it is a Sunday, the planetary hours will start on the Sun and continue in sequence, meaning that it would look like this:

Hour	Planet
1	Sun
2	Venus
3	Mercury
4	Moon
5	Saturn
6	Jupiter
7	Mars
8	Sun
9	Venus
10	Mercury
11	Moon
12	Saturn

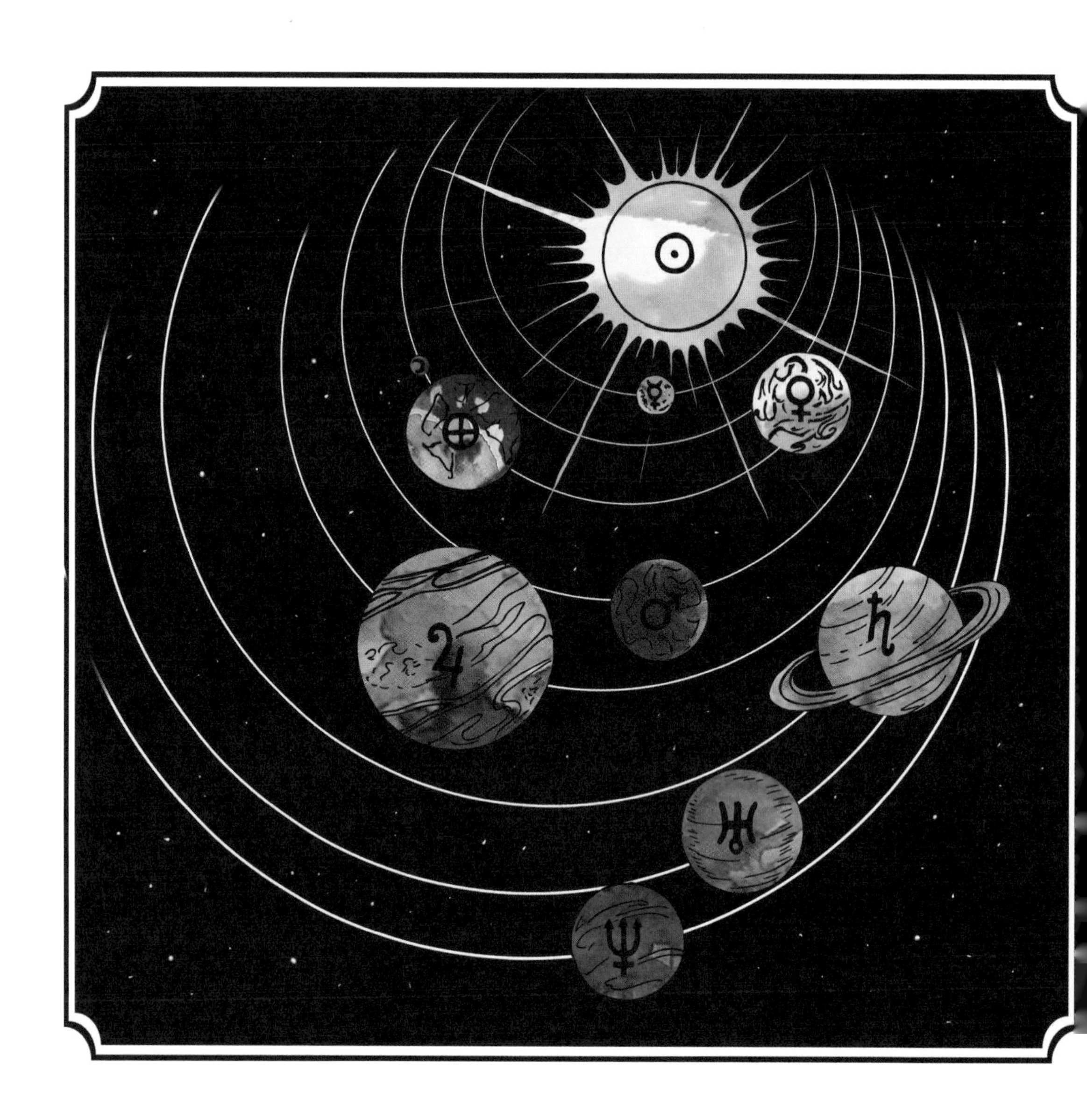

As you can see in the table, the Venus hour will be the second and the ninth hour. We want to cast the spell in the morning, so we choose the second. On that day, the day hours last 52 minutes, so it will start (52 x 1) minutes after the sunrise and end (52 x 2) minutes after the sunrise. Translated to our usual hours, this means that the Venus hour that day starts at 9:28 and ends at 10:20.

Planetary Positions

Finally, the position and movement of planets in the sky can also affect magickal workings and other aspects of our daily lives. The position of celestial bodies in the sky will determine their areas of influence, and the correspondences of said celestial bodies will determine how they affect us.

To know the position of the celestial bodies, we need to dig into the origin of the signs of the zodiac. It is rooted in the constellations that can be seen in a certain part of the sky, defined by the path of the sun across the sky seen from the Earth. This zone is called the zodiac belt, and there you can find the twelve constellations that give name to the zodiac signs. As the orbits of the planets are almost in the same plane, the paths of the moon and visible planets are within the belt of the zodiac. As they move, they pass through the different signs and associate them with different energies.

The movement of the planets is also an aspect to keep in mind in astrology. You may have heard about retrograde planets, particularly Mercury retrograde. When a planet is in retrograde, that means that it appears to be moving backward in the night sky. This is due to the different speed of the orbit of the planets around the sun; think of it like when you pass a slower car on the road.

Retrograde planets have different correspondences and connotations in astrology. The retrograde phase is a cycle, and it is repeated after a set time for each planet.

There are many astrological sources of influence. To help you keep track of them, there are calendars, journals, and mobile apps available.

Moon Phases and the Thirteen Moons of the Year

The moon has been a strong presence in the spirituality of many ancient religions, being seen as a feminine symbol or a goddess. This connection may be motivated by the fact that the moon takes about twenty-eight days to complete its cycle, the same number of days as the average menstrual cycle.

Through tides, the moon exhibits all her influence on our planet and the life on it. It was believed that the moon phases also affected our lives by interfering with the chemistry of our bodies. However, this theory has been dismissed.

I think that it is important to understand the science behind the moon phases, why the moon affects tides, and why its cycle takes twenty-eight days. If you don't feel drawn to learning these kinds of things, there are simple ways to keep track of the moon phases, including moon calendars and mobile apps that even allow you to set alarms for certain phases.

The moon has always been strongly related to witchcraft. Its energy affects us and teaches us the lessons of growing, letting go, and waiting for the appropriate moment. Each phase is related to a different type of energy. This makes one phase more suitable than the rest when casting spells that involve that type energy. Casting a spell under an inadequate moon phase won't make it fail, but it will make it less powerful than what it could be if you cast it with the right timing.

Each moon phase represents a specific mindset as you move forward and achieve your aims, teaching us lessons about cycles and balance.

New Moon

As the moon starts a new cycle, so do we. The new moon is the moment to get rid of what no longer serves you. It is a moment of rebirth, fresh starts, and new projects. Set your goals and intentions for the future phases. Rituals related to the new moon include the following:

- New beginnings
- Looking for new jobs
- Sending your intentions to the universe
- Focusing and grounding yourself

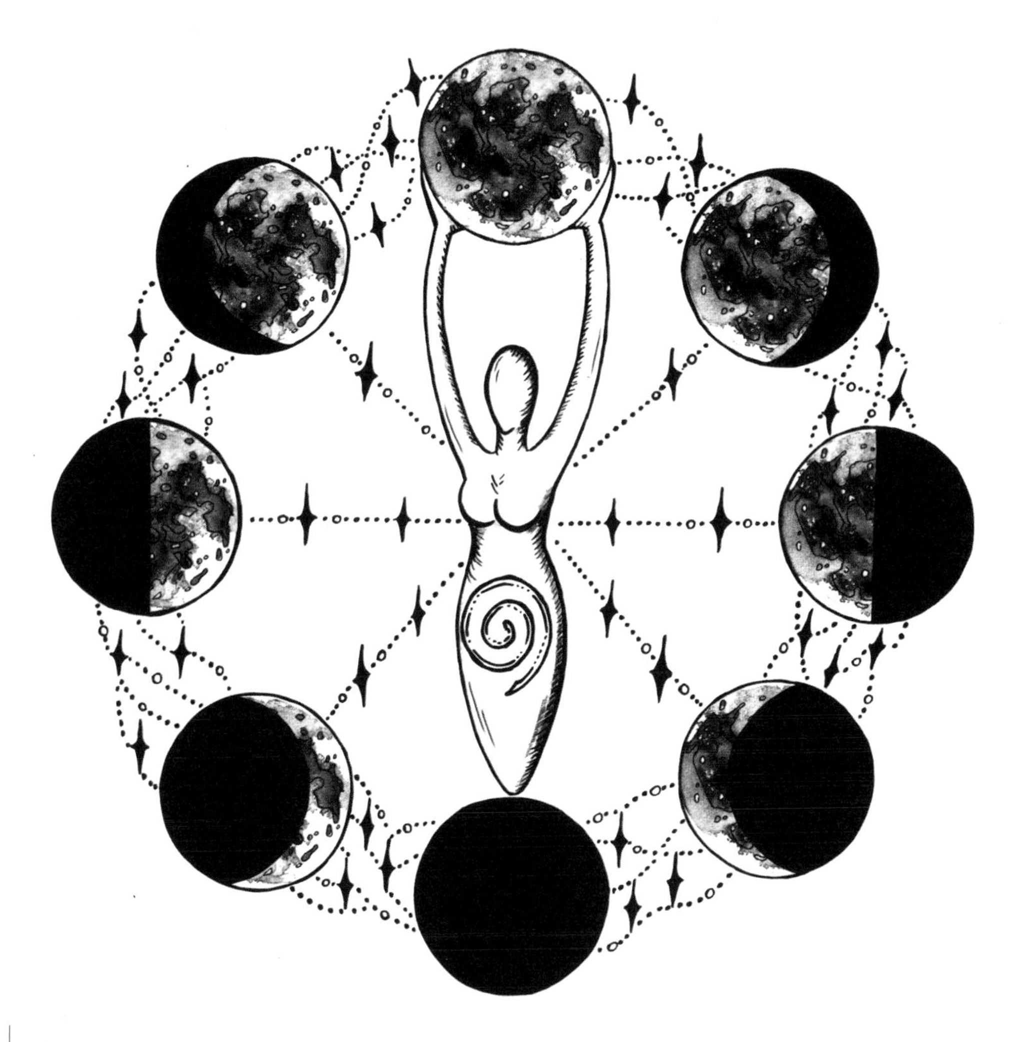

Waxing Crescent Moon

Once you have defined your objectives, it is time to organize yourself to achieve them. The waxing crescent teaches us that to achieve our goals we need to do adequate research and planning. Appropriate spells and rituals include the following:

- Finding lost things
- Bringing what you want into your life
- Abundance, money, or career spells
- Visualization

First Quarter Moon

The first quarter moon teaches us that once we have everything ready it is time to start working toward our goals. To achieve them, we need to put in hard work. This moon phase is the necessary initial boost of energy. It is the perfect moment for the following:

- Energizing spells
- Growing your inner energy
- Making decisions
- Finding issues and flaws in your planning and taking actions to correct them

Waxing Gibbous Moon

This phase is about focus. We need to accept that all of our goals may not be achievable, and we need to concentrate our efforts on those that are. Time and energy management are an important part of life if we want to keep balance. Focus your spells and rituals in this phase on the following:

- Success in all types of projects
- Seeking guidance
- Manifestation rituals
- Keeping balance

Full Moon

This phase was once believed to alter mental states and promote mental instability. Remember the stories of werewolves that transformed during the full moon or how the word *lunatic* means "crazy." Nowadays, witches consider full moons a moment of high power, when our intuition is more active.

While some of us feel energized and enjoy working under the full moon, others may feel overwhelmed, have problems sleeping, and be too active. The full moon tells us that this is our time for blooming and harvesting the results of our hard work and efforts. This phase is particularly related to the following:

- Goal manifestation
- Psychic abilities and divination
- Love spells and strengthening bonds
- Cleansing and recharging tools
- Making moon water

Waning Gibbous Moon

This phase emphasizes gratitude. Let yourself enjoy what you have achieved. Shared happiness is the best happiness, so surround yourself with your loved ones and enjoy the nurturing environment. The rituals and spells that match this time include the following:

- Gratitude spells
- Spells to protect or better your relationship with your family
- Letting go of guilt and regrets
- Self-knowledge

Last Quarter Moon

This phase is about burdens and baggage. Let go of what is toxic or draining your energy. Get rid of the energy that is preventing you from moving forward so that you can continue walking your path and growing. Here are some rituals and spells you can try:

- Deep cleansing and detox rituals
- Protection spells
- Karma/justice spells
- Banishing spells

Waning Crescent Moon

The lesson from this phase is that after all the hard work we all need a time to rest and recharge ourselves. Don't overwork yourself. Resting is a necessary step to restart the cycle. This is the perfect time for the following:

- Resting and recharging yourself
- Forgiveness and self-forgiveness
- Self-reflecting rituals
- Journaling

Keep in mind that moon phases match their timing in both hemispheres, but it is oriented differently. This means that the moon increases its phase in opposite directions. For example, a waxing moon in the northern hemisphere has the shape of the letter D, while in the southern hemisphere it will be shaped like the letter C.

Naming the Moon

Moons phases were also a way to count time. For example, ancient Celts used a calendar with thirteen months that followed the thirteen full moons that are in a year. Ancient European and North American traditions also gave names to each of the full moons, linking them with the events and cycles in nature at that time of the year. Because these names where developed by people in the northern hemisphere, they match northern seasons and not the ones of the southern hemisphere. Some witches still follow these traditions.

Here are the most popular names for each moon:

WOLF MOON The first moon of the year is named after the wolves that howl during this time as the mating season approaches. They can be heard clearly in the silence of the winter.

SNOW MOON The February full moon is known as the Snow Moon because of the weather during this month. Some North American tribes called it the Hunger Moon, as the food reserves from the harvest where usually running low and there is not much to eat during winter.

WORM MOON The full moon in March alludes to the worms that start appearing in the soil as the spring comes closer. It is a message of hope that Mother Nature is waking up from her winter sleep.

PINK MOON The moon in April is strongly related to the color of the new flowers that start blooming. It is also known as the Grass Moon.

FLOWER MOON But if there is a full moon strongly related to flowers, then it's the May moon. It is also called the Milk Moon because the sheep and cows reach maximum milk production.

STRAWBERRY MOON The moon of the month of June is related to all the berries that are ripe and ready to eat.

BUCK MOON July's moon alludes to the deer bucks and the new antlers that start to emerge on their foreheads. It is also called the Thunder Moon because of the thunderstorms that are frequent during this time of the year.

STURGEON MOON Sturgeons are a type of fish that live in lakes and were fished during August by Native Americans, giving the full moon in this month its name.

HARVEST MOON This is also known as the Corn Moon, with both names being related to the September harvest.

HUNTER MOON As the October harvest is finishing, it is time to store food to survive the winter. This includes hunting for meat, which names this full moon.

BEAVER MOON November's moon is also related to hunting because this was the last occasion to set up traps for beavers to use their meat and fur.

COLD MOON The last moon of the year announces that winter has arrived and the nights will quickly become longer and darker.

Because the cycle of the moon lasts less than the standard length of a month, some years this discrepancy is compensated by two full moons in the same month. When this happens, the second full moon is called a Blue Moon.

Spells and Rituals

Sometimes people use the words *spell* and *ritual* interchangeably, but the terms do not mean the same thing. Spells are usually simpler: you channel your energy to create a subtle change in the universe that allows you to achieve a specific goal. Rituals are usually more long lasting, and their objective is not always to create change. A ritual can also be about celebrating something, such as a birth or a ceremony of handfasting. Rituals may also be a way to express your gratitude to a deity or your ancestors. A spell can be a central part of a ritual, but not all rituals contain spells.

Cleansing

Cleansing is a ritual to remove unwanted energies attached to your magickal tools. It should be done regularly. Do it when you first get your item and after every time you use it. There are some items that I like to cleanse before using them as well.

Unwanted energies are a common thing, and it doesn't mean that something bad happened to your tools. Think about it as cleaning something, like clothing. It gets dirty if you wear it, and it needs to be washed before using it again, but that does not mean that it can't be used anymore. You should take special care when cleansing something that belonged to someone before you. It is likely that it has attached energy from the previous owner.

Everything that is alive has vital energy within it. This includes people. It is also important to cleanse ourselves regularly, as all types of energies can be attached to our bodies.

Spaces can also accumulate unwanted energies. It is important to cleanse your house regularly, especially if you plan on casting a spell or feel a negative buildup. When cleansing a space, it is often advised to open your windows and doors to allow negative energy to get out.

There are many different cleansing techniques, but they are all rooted in the same principles: disrupting and eliminating the energy linked to an object, a person, or a space. Some cleansing methods can cause damage; research them before using them. Smoke, moonlight, and sound cleansing methods are usually safe for most objects.

Water

Water is a great cleansing agent—especially water from natural sources such as rain, rivers, and springs. You can also bless water from a human source and use it for cleansing. Some of the most popular ways of water cleansing are submerging objects in blessed water, taking ritual baths, and sprinkling water on an area or object. Some witches like to add herbs, essential oils, salt, or other ingredients to their cleansing water.

Salt

Its energy-absorbing properties make salt one of the most valued cleansing methods. It can be used in combination with water, but objects should be rinsed with clean water afterward, as salt can leave a residue. Be careful: Salt, and especially saltwater, can make some metals rust.

Soil

When we use soil or bury an object to cleanse it, we are asking Mother Earth to help us eliminate the negative energy. She absorbs this energy into her body and changes it, imbuing the object with neutral and grounding energy. Negative energy does not hurt Mother Earth—what does hurt her is human pollution. For this reason, it is important to make sure that the object that you plan on burying is safe for animals and plants. If it is not safe, gather a bit of soil and place it in a bowl to use it for cleansing purposes.

Fire

This technique is very powerful; however, it is not widely used because it damages most objects. Fire can be a force of destruction, but also of creation. Wildfires can quickly burn forests, but some tree species are adapted to them and their seeds spread better after a forest fire, creating new life. By placing an object in a fire, we renew its energy.

Smoke

Smoke cleansing combines the elements fire and air in one cleansing technique. It has roots in several ancient civilizations, each one of them using herbs that grew where they were located. Not all herbs are suitable for smoke cleansing. My advice is to create your own personal herb blend for different occasions. Some of the most commonly used herbs for this purpose are cedar, cypress, rosemary, lavender, and thyme. To burn the herbs, use a small piece of charcoal and a fireproof container if the herbs are loose or make herb bundles. To cleanse an object with smoke, hold the item with your projecting hand and pass it through the smoke, allowing it to envelop the object. Please, keep in mind that smoke can be harmful for most pets.

Natural Light

Sunlight and moonlight are used for cleansing and charging purposes. Just place what you want to cleanse outdoors and let the light bathe it. Some witches like to synchronize their cleansing cycles with the solar or lunar cycle. It is common to use this technique along with soil or water, by placing the object under the light in contact with the earth or some water.

Sound

This technique tends to be overlooked, but it is one of my favorites, particularly to cleanse spaces. Have you noticed how the mood of a space can change by playing a positive song? That is sound cleansing. Some more advanced techniques include bells, percussion, singing bowls, and even clapping.

Charging

Cleansing transforms the negative or unwanted energy from a space, object, or person into a more neutral one. To use objects, we need to imbue them with wanted energy, and for that we use an external source of energy. Choose a source that fits your craft, but that doesn't harm what is being charged.

Common Charging Methods

YOUR INNER ENERGY This is the most important charging technique of all. By using your own energy, you ensure that the aim of the item is set on fulfilling your intention.

NATURAL LIGHT Sunlight and moonlight cleanse and charge items at the same time, so this method allows you to save some time. Keep in mind that sunlight can damage items, in particular crystals.

FIRE This method is a bit different from the rest because its aim is usually to consume what you want to charge, releasing the magick within it. For example, it is common to burn a piece of paper with your goal or a sigil (page 161) on it to activate it. Fire is also incorporated in rituals that require a candle to burn down completely to charge an item or cast a spell.

PENTACLE PLATE Lay your object on a pentacle plate with representation of each element in its corresponding point on the star. Visualize the energy of the elements going inside it and charging it.

CRYSTAL GRIDS Place the item that you want to charge in the center and surround it with crystals, creating a pattern (see "Crystal Grids" on page 86). Some crystals are more suitable for this than others. For example, selenite and clear quartz are very popular for this method. You can also match the properties of the crystal with the item that you want to charge. For example, amethyst boosts psychic abilities, so it can be used to charge divination tools.

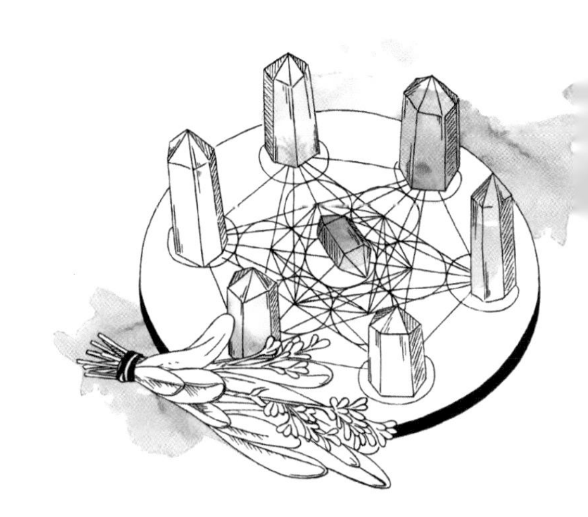

Casting a Circle

When you cast a spell or perform a ritual, you want to make sure that the energy from your surroundings doesn't disturb it. You also want to keep the energy that you are raising contained in your workspace. Circles are a sacred symbol that represents protection by delimiting our space. They also symbolize time and its repeating cycles.

Not all witchcraft branches cast circles, and the ones that do have different traditions and rituals to cast them even if the theory behind them is the same. This method is the one I use, but feel free to modify it or research your own.

MARK A CIRCLE The circle is traditionally drawn with salt, but it can be done with sand, crystals, or simply visualization. Keep in mind not to use salt outdoors, as it harms plants and small animals.

MARK THE ELEMENTS Starting on the east and continuing clockwise, place a representation of each one of the four elements at its corresponding cardinal point. (See chapter 2, page 17.)

- East – Air
- North – Earth
- West – Water
- South – Fire

Invoke them with your voice while you do so. If you work with deities, this is also the time to invoke them.

RAISE AND PROJECT YOUR ENERGY, DELIMITING THE CIRCLE Start at the east and continue clockwise. Visualize your energy as a line of light that only allows the passage of the energy that you want involved in your ritual or spell.

CLEANSE AND BLESS THE SPACE Use the technique of your choosing (page 156).

Now you can start to perform your magickal workings. Once you have finished, remember to thank the elements and your deities before dismissing them.

Moon Water

Moon water is a valuable ingredient in many spells because it imbues them with the energy of the moon. It is also commonly used to cleanse and charge magickal tools with the power of the moon.

To make moon water, fill a transparent container with water. A glass jar works well for this. Place it where the moonlight can reach it for the entire night. Gather it before sunrise and store it in a dark place. And that's it!

Keep the following in mind:

- You can still make moon water if it is a cloudy night. Place the container where the moonlight would normally reach. The energy is still there.
- Some witches like to make moon water from the different moon phases because they have different correspondences (page 151). However, the full moon is the most commonly used phase.
- If you plan to use the moon water for drinking, cooking, or making potions, be sure to use safe drinking water. For other uses, you can take water from natural sources. Keep in mind that this kind of water can spoil if it is not stored adequately in the fridge. Label your moon water with the date and the phase of the moon.
- Be careful during winter. If your container is too full and closed, it can break if the water inside freezes.

Some witches also enjoy making sun water. The process is the same as for moon water except it's made during daytime.

Candle Magick

Candles have a central spot in witchcraft, as they are included in many spells and rituals. They incorporate the element of fire into our magick, allowing us to send our intentions into the web of the universe.

Candles can be incorporated to perform more complex rituals. Here are some steps for a simple spell.

1. Choose the right candle. Each color and scent is used to express a set intent. The candle that you use should match your intention. If you can't find the right one, use a white candle.
2. Cleanse your working space and the candle. Carve your intention in the candle. A boline (page 39) is traditionally used for this.
3. Bless the candle and anoint it with oils and herbs that also match your intention. While you do this, charge the candle with your intention.
4. Place the candle on your altar in a place where you can safely light it. Some witches like to create a circle of salt or crystals around their candles.
5. Light the candle and while it burns concentrate on your intention. Meditate about it or repeat it as a mantra. Some spells may require you to repeat your intention a certain number of times, linking them to numerology. Once you feel that your intention has been sent to the universe, close the spell. Some of the most common phrases for this are "so mote it be" or "this spell is cast."
6. Let the candle burn completely. The spell is cast, but usually the candle needs to burn completely. Do not leave it unattended while it is still burning.

Sigils

A sigil is a symbol created to represent a goal or desire. This kind of magick is versatile because it can be used to manifest almost any intention.

You can find predesigned sigils, but my advice is to create your own. The more personal the sigil is, the better. There are many different ways to design sigils, but the magick behind them and how they are used is the same.

1. ESTABLISH YOUR INTENT As with every other spell, the intention for your sigil should be realistic and positively phrased. Personally, I like to use short and concise sentences, and I avoid attaching more than one goal to a sigil.

2. SIMPLIFY YOUR INTENT Strike out all the vowels and duplicated consonants. If when you do this you end up with only three letters or less, try to rephrase your intention.

3. DESIGN THE SIGIL A basic sigil design is very popular due to its simplicity. Simplify the remaining letters to the most basic strokes, like straight lines, circles, or curved lines. A witch's sigil wheel is useful when you have more complex words or sentences. Trace the words, connecting the letters in order. Usually, each word is traced separately, starting with a dot and ending with a line or an arrow. If your intention is short, you can trace it all together.

4. CREATE THE DESIGN Play with the strokes, arranging them in different ways until you find a design that you like. Change their placement and size until they don't resemble the initial letters anymore.

5. CHARGE AND FORGET THE SIGIL Once your design is ready, it's time to give it real power. Meditate with your sigil in your projective hand to infuse it with your intention. If you want to achieve a certain feeling, focus on past experiences when you felt it. Keep in mind that what you are charging is the design itself, not the piece of paper on which it is written. Allow the sentence that originates it to disappear and only remember the idea or the feeling behind the sigil. This will connect your subconscious with the sigil.

6. RELEASE THE SIGIL Once the sigil is charged, it is time to release it back to the universe. The most common way to do this is by burning it; this way, you free it from its physical form and allow the energy to start working. Now you can forget about it and just let it do its thing.

After these steps, some witches like to reuse their sigils by putting them in places relevant to their meaning. For example, you can place a protective sigil in the soles of your shoes to walk home safely, or you can put a self-love sigil in your water bottle. But sigils should be released once their work has ended (either the spell has worked or not).

In addition to creating sigils with sentences and letters, you can make sigils with drawings and pictograms related to its intention. There are many other ways to create sigils; you just need to find the one that feels right for you and then practice.

Glamours

Glamours are a specific type of spell that focuses on creating an illusion, particularly in the way you are seen by others. They are the typical beauty spells, but they are more versatile than that. You can also cast a glamour to go unnoticed (sometimes called "invisibility glamours") or to attract more attention.

It is important to keep in mind that glamours don't create physical changes; you can think about them as the "makeup" of magick. Because of this, it is usually more useful to cast them with an intent related to a personal trait rather than one related to physical appearance. For example, "I want to look more attractive" is more likely to work than "I want to be more beautiful."

This type of spell is usually cast over an object that you can wear when you need the effect to manifest. For example, it is very popular to cast a glamour over a lipstick to look more confident. The glamour will be active while you wear that lipstick.

Color correspondences are strongly related to glamours. If you want to cast a glamour over a hoodie to go unnoticed, it's better to choose a black hoodie than a bright orange one. Similarly, if you want to cast a spell to seem more approachable on a perfume bottle, choose a sweet scent rather than a stronger one.

To cast a glamour over an item, you just need to charge it with your intention. You can also include crystals while you cast it to boost its effect.

Another popular way to cast glamours, particularly those related to attractiveness or self-confidence, is through ritual baths and lotions. Ritual baths with crystals and herbs allow you to recharge yourself with the energy of the glamour, while the lotion covers your body and allows you to absorb its effects.

Amulets and Talismans

Amulets and talismans may seem like the same thing, and the truth is that they share some similarities. Amulets are small objects that have set magickal associations due to their nature. They are commonly used to attract good things. For example, a four-leaf clover is used to attract good luck and a shiny coin can be used to attract money. They work better when they are worn or carried by their owner.

Talismans are more intricate and bigger objects, usually designed with a magickal goal in mind. They have more specific goals than amulets, and they improve your abilities in a particular field. Because they are bigger, they usually can be carried but not worn.

Charms

Charms are small objects that need to be charged with your intention in order to work. To create a charm, choose a small object related to your intention as well as a candle with the right color correspondence. Carve your intention on the candle with your boline. Place the charm under the candle and light the candle. Focus on meditating on your intention. Let the fire channel it and charge your charm. Be careful with the fire, as your charm can be damaged by this process.

Another technique to create charms is knot magick. With every knot, you seal your intention. This can be useful to create protective bracelets with strings, but it can also be applied to knitting or other handcrafts.

Witch's Ladders

A popular knot magick spell is a witch's ladder. These are usually for long-term spells, and they can be used as meditation tools and as a way to cast spells.

To make one, you need three pieces of rope each about 3 feet (1 m) long and nine items (feathers, crystals, shells, other charms, etc.). Choose colors that match your intent.

Clear your mind and focus on your intent. Line up your three strands and knot them at the top to make a loop so you can hang it. Start braiding them and knotting the items, trying to leave the same length between one item and the next.

This traditional chant is used to help you raise your energy and send it to the ladder:

"By knot of one, the spell's begun.
By knot of two, the magick comes true.
By knot of three, so it shall be.
By knot of four, this power is stored.
By knot of five, my will shall drive.
By knot of six, the spell I fix.
By knot of seven, the future I leaven.
By knot of eight, my will be fate.
By knot of nine, what is done is mine."

Each time you're making a knot you're securing the spell. Once the ladder is complete, the spell is cast, but you can use it to meditate when you feel it needs reinforcement.

Things I Wish Someone Had Told Me

Skills Can Be Learned

One of the questions I get asked the most is: "I don't have any special skills. How can I practice witchcraft?" This is a misconception of witchcraft that is widespread. The truth is that you don't need to be born with any special skill.

It is true that some people have talents that make some aspects of the craft easier or more natural for them. However, with effort, you can master all these abilities. Research what you want to learn. Read reliable sources, and gather information to help you put the techniques into practice. Think about it like learning how to paint and draw. You need to study anatomy, perspective, colors, and so on, and then you need to practice a lot. But if you persevere, you will master it.

Also remember that most people who say that don't have any skill really do have one, but they haven't discovered it yet. The more you learn, and the more you practice, the easier it will be for you to discover your hidden skills.

The Thirteen Zodiacs

In the zodiac belt, you can find the twelve constellations that give name to the twelve zodiac signs. There is a thirteenth main constellation in this belt named Ophiuchus. Located between Scorpius and Sagittarius, Ophiuchus was left out of the zodiac signs in the fifth century when Babylonians divided the year into twelve months and made them match the zodiac signs.

Ophiuchus is depicted as a man grabbing a snake. It is said to be mysterious like Scorpio but also adventurous like Sagittarius. Some modern zodiac systems have included it, assigning it the dates from November 29 to December 17.

Common Mistakes

Spells and rituals do not always work. This is more common than you might think! If this happens to you, don't worry. Check how you cast your spell. Pay attention to the astrological events that were occurring and the environment that surrounded you. This is when a witchcraft journal comes in handy. With this information, you will be better able to discover what went wrong and fix it. Plus, it will allow you to monitor your progress.

These are some of the most common mistakes:

WANTING TO CAST SPELLS TOO SOON Some people are naturally born with skills that allow them to cast spells with little to no training and research. Most of us aren't like that. Understanding and working on your inner energy is a necessary step, and eventually you will be able to project it. Also, research allows you to walk the witchcraft path safely and obtain more accurate and powerful changes.

NOT GETTING YOUR INTENTION RIGHT Defining your intention can be one of the hardest parts of casting a spell, and it can take several days of preparation work before you are actually ready to cast it. Once you have a realistic goal, ask yourself whether this is what you really want or whether there is another reason behind it. For example, do you really want to move, or do you want your neighbors to be less noisy?

HAVING UNREALISTIC EXPECTATIONS Yes, witchcraft allows us to create changes that may seem unbelievable for some people, but it is linked to the laws of nature. Don't be misled by how the media portrays witchcraft and its effects.

LETTING NEGATIVE EMOTIONS DEFINE YOUR SPELL Word your intention as something positive instead of negative. This will help it work and help you achieve your goal. For example, instead of stating "I don't want to fail," try "I want to succeed." There is an exception to this rule, as some spells aimed to hurt other people, such as hexes and curses, feed on strong negative energies. However, I discourage the use of these types of spells.

GIVING IN TO SELF-DOUBT Change starts from the inside. If you believe that your spell won't work, it won't work. Don't self-sabotage your progress. You have the power within you. Believe in yourself.

NOT WORKING FOR IT Spells are a great help, but if you don't do your part, they usually don't work. For example, if you cast a spell to find a job but you don't send out your résumé to any companies, chances are that the spell will fail. Once you cast a spell, keep working in the mundane world to achieve your goals.

OTHER FORCES WORKING AGAINST YOU Sometimes forces more powerful than our own are working against our desires and preventing our spells from succeeding. When this happens, investigate what is blocking your actions and, if you can, address that issue first.

Keep in mind that your spell may be working in a different way than you expected. Sometimes the universe fulfills our requests following a path different from the one that we planned or anticipated. This does not mean that your spell has failed. On the contrary, it has been a success. Adapt to the new situation and be grateful because your goal has been achieved.

Don't let mistakes or fear of making mistakes discourage you from trying to cast spells. Practice is also an important part of success. Just keep in mind that knowledge and practice take time. You may have some failed spells before you find success. Remember: A witch is always learning.

Questions to Ask Yourself Before Casting a Spell

A successful spell begins with you. Ask yourself these questions first to make sure you are ready to cast your spell.

- **Is my intention well defined?** You need to find the reason behind your first impulse to cast a spell, and make sure that it is achievable. Once you have determined it, define it in a concise, positive way.
- **Do I understand the potential consequences of this intention and spell?** When spells work, they always create a change. Be aware of the effects that your spell can have on the lives of others. Plus, there is always the risk that your spell may backfire. Think ahead.
- **Does my intention contradict my morals?** As with all of your actions, you are responsible for the consequences of your spell.
- **If you haven't designed it, does it need to be modified?** Sometimes, if we follow the steps of a spell that is not ours, it may not completely adapt to our situation. Changing some ingredients or steps to make it fit your situation will help you achieve your goals.
- **Am I ready to work toward my goal in the mundane world?** Avoid the common mistake of expecting witchcraft to take care of everything. Spells give you a helping hand toward your goals, but they don't do all the work.

Come Back

Acknowledgments

To all who have accompanied me during this journey, making this dream possible.

Disclaimer

This book was designed to be as complete as possible given its limited space. Its main objective is to inform and entertain; however, it does not replace professional services. Consult a professional when needed. Some countries may have regulations that interfere with what is said in this book; please comply with them.

The author and publisher are not responsible for any loss or damage caused, directly or indirectly, by the contents of this book.

About the Author

Lidia Pradas is the Wiccan witch behind the Instagram sensation Wiccan Tips. She was born in Spain and comes from a family of witches who taught her Celtic pagan traditions. Lidia writes and teaches about witchcraft and paganism, and she is dedicated to helping beginner witches find their own Wiccan path.

INDEX

D

E

F